Curing Exceptionalism

What's wrong with how we think about the United States?

What can we do about it?

by David Swanson

Charlottesville, VA
First edition—2018

Also by David Swanson
WAR IS NEVER JUST (2016)
WAR IS A LIE (2010, 2016)
KILLING IS NOT A WAY OF LIFE (2014)
WAR NO MORE: THE CASE FOR ABOLITION (2013)
IRAQ WAR AMONG WORLD'S WORST EVENTS (2013)
TUBE WORLD (2012)
THE MILITARY INDUSTRIAL COMPLEX AT 50 (2011)
WHEN THE WORLD OUTLAWED WAR (2011)
DAYBREAK: UNDOING THE IMPERIAL PRESIDENCY
AND FORMING A MORE PERFECT UNION (2009)
THE 35 ARTICLES OF IMPEACHMENT (Introduction, 2008)
davidswanson.org

• • •

Swanson, David, 1969 Dec. 1-

Curing Exceptionalism

Book design by David Swanson.

Printed in the USA
First Edition / April 2018
ISBN: 978-0-9980859-3-7

Past Praise for the Author's Work

"David Swanson is a truth-teller and witness-bearer whose voice and action warrant our attention." —Cornel West, author.

"David Swanson predicates his belief that nonviolence can change the world on careful research and historical analysis." —Kathy Kelly, activist and author.

"The world needs more true advocates of democracy like David Swanson!" —Thom Hartmann, radio/TV host and author.

"Our times cry out for a smart, witty and courageous Populist who hasn't forgotten how to play offense. Luckily we have David Swanson." —Mike Ferner, activist and author.

"David Swanson, who has been a one-man wonder leading the charge for accountability, writes a compelling narrative that inspires not just outrage, but ACTION." —Medea Benjamin, activist and author.

"David Swanson despises war and lying, and unmasks them both with rare intelligence. I learn something new on every page." —Jeff Cohen, activist and author.

"Swanson's book is far more uplifting and inspiring than virtually any other book in its genre, as it devotes itself to laying out a detailed plan for how American citizens—through the activism to which he has devoted himself—can bring about a rejuvenation of our political values." —Glenn Greenwald, author.

"David Swanson is the most consistently great writer of this generation." —Jean Athey, activist.

"David Swanson is an antidote to the toxins of complacency and evasion. He insists on rousing the sleepwalkers, confronting the deadly prevaricators and shining a bright light on possibilities for a truly better world." —Norman Solomon, activist and author.

"I am always impressed and inspired by David's prolific energy and I admire his unwavering opposition to *all war*, not just the ones started or continued by Republicans." —Cindy Sheehan, activist and author.

"David Swanson writes like he talks; that is to say, in clear, sharp language that gets to the root of the issue, but in a very personal way...as if you are having a one-on-one conversation with him." —Leah Bolger, activist.

The author, being arrested at the White House.

CONTENTS

INTRODUCTION

U.S. exceptionalism, the idea that the United States of America is superior to other nations, is no more fact-based and no less harmful than racism, sexism, and other forms of bigotry. The purpose of this book is to persuade you of that statement.

The first section of the book is a glorified list of statistics with minimal discussion. Its purpose is to examine as fairly and honestly as possible, with the most reliable data available, how the United States compares with other nations.

Is what is often called the "greatest nation on earth" actually greatest in any measurable category? Is it, in fact, the least great in some ways? Is it, in many ways, just kind of average? I think it's important that we first learn these facts and only afterwards discuss them -- even if the more popular order of operations may be just the reverse.

Having established some knowledge of how the United States actually compares with other countries, we'll move on in part two to an examination of how exceptionalists think, relying heavily on their own words. Exceptionalist thinking turns out to have rather little to do with facts, and a great deal to do with an arrogant attitude.

In the third section of the book, I argue that this attitude is not harmless, that in fact it brings a great deal of suffering to both those who engage in it and those impacted by it. Given this understanding, I am compelled to attempt in the book's fourth and final part to suggest what I see as the most promising steps for curing exceptionalism, for developing better ways of thinking and for taking the actions those new thoughts lead to.

I. How the United States Compares with Other Countries

The United States in geographic size is much smaller than Russia, a little smaller than Europe if Europe is treated as one whole, and by most calculations slightly smaller than Canada or China. The United States is significantly bigger than Brazil or Australia, and dramatically bigger than each of some 200 other countries, including each separate country of Europe.[1]

The United States in population size is dramatically smaller than China or India but significantly larger than every other country on earth.[2]

Because the United States is larger in both area and population than most countries, it's important to look not just at straightforward comparisons but also at per-square-mile and per-capita comparisons whenever relevant and possible.

The U.S. ranks as the top publisher of rankings, hands down. So it's important to look at both U.S. and any non-U.S. sources of rankings that can be found.

Although many in the United States like to think of it as holding first place in many admirable categories, it's hard to actually find a category where this is true. Perhaps the most popular claim is on behalf of "freedom." The United States is said to be the most "free." But virtually no study, from any political perspective, actually makes that finding.

The British-based Legatum Institute, which ranks the United States 18th in overall "prosperity," ranks it 28th in "personal freedom."[3] The U.S.-based Cato Institute ranks the United States 24th in "personal freedom" and 11th in "economic freedom."[4] The Canadian-based World Freedom Index ranks the United States 27th in a combined consideration of "economic," "political," and "press" freedoms.[5] The U.S.-government-funded Freedom House ranks the United States 16th in "civil liberties."[6] The French-based Reporters Without Borders ranks the United States 43rd in "press freedom."[7] The U.S.-based Heritage Foundation ranks the United States 18th in "economic freedom."[8] The Spanish-based World Index of Moral Freedom ranks the United States 7th.[9] The British-based *Economist Magazine*'s Democracy Index has the United States in a three-way tie for 20th place.[10] The CIA-funded Polity Data Series gives the U.S. democracy a score of 8 out of 10, but gives 58 other countries a higher score.[11]

Some of these sources' conceptions of freedom are at odds with each other, as well as with my own conception of a good society. The point is that virtually nobody, on the left or the right or anywhere else, ranks the United States as the leader in liberty, by any definition -- not even in the "economic liberty" of capitalism. Related, albeit inversely, to freedom is incarceration, where the United States does rank first in overall number of prisoners, and in per-capita rate of imprisonment (with the possible exception of the Seychelles Islands).[12]

Among those who have looked seriously into such matters and still claimed first place for the United States in some admirable category, the most common category is probably "top-ranked" or "research" universities. It is perhaps not as grand a claim as "Land of the Free," but "land of the good universities" is still a nice title.

The United States is indeed often ranked as having the most overall, and the most top-ranked universities in the world. But both claims are false if a per-capita comparison is used. The United States has also been ranked as producing the most doctoral degrees (PhDs), though that, too, isn't true per capita.[13] All such numerical comparisons are of limited value, of course. For example, we'd probably be better off if certain for-profit, non-educational, debt-trap universities did *not* exist. And a majority of supporters of the Republican Party tell the Pew Research Center that higher education as a whole has a negative impact.[14] Providing a hint at divisions within, the United States may have both the most PhDs and the most people who believe college is bad for you.

Nonetheless, numbers are a place to start, and there do seem to exist some credible numbers related to universities declared by various sources to be "top-ranked." Rankings from the United States[15], United Kingdom[16], and China[17] all place the U.S. first in most universities in the top 100, but ninth or tenth in the same measurement per capita. Countries that lead the U.S. in at least one study in most universities in the top 100 per capita are Australia, Belgium, Denmark, Finland, Hong Kong, Netherlands, Norway, Singapore, Sweden, Switzerland, and the United Kingdom.

Having the most top universities is certainly significant, and even ranking ninth or tenth in having the most top universities per capita is pretty darn good. Of course, these calculations do not tell us the quality of the lower-ranked universities that most students attend. Nor do they consider the sizes of the universities or the moral character of what is taught in them. They certainly do not consider the cost of the universities or the debt that typical students find themselves in after attending. The

United States leads the world in student debt,[18] while dozens of countries offer free university educations. And the United States has slipped from first place to now trail several other countries in per-capita college graduation rate.[19] So one can cheer for the rankings won by top U.S. universities, but a U.S. student is less likely to actually attend any university, and more likely -- if he or she does attend -- to emerge burdened with tremendous debt.

YAY, NUMBER ONE!

Of course, it would be odd for a country near the top in population and area not to rank #1 in some things, and having the most top-ranked universities is a pretty good one. But it does matter to the quality of life in the United States that it is not in first place in a per capita comparison. One way to judge the quality of much of the university education in the United States, and the education of those millions of students who do not attend universities, is to look at primary and secondary education, where the United States ranks mediocre at best. The Programme for

International Student Assessment (PISA) ranks U.S. students 38th out of 71 countries in math and 24th in both science and reading.[20] The Trends in International Mathematics and Science Study (TIMSS) ranks U.S. students in tenth place or lower in every category (both math and science in both fourth and eighth grades) out of 50 some countries looked at in each case.[21]

So, perhaps the United States is not a clear-cut world leader in freedom or education, but surely there must be something else admirable that it leads in, right? Well, there's the Olympic medal count, although it doesn't hold up under a per capita comparison or a geographic area comparison,[22] and it may be slipping away. In the 2018 winter olympics, three nations, all with much smaller populations, picked up more medals than did the United States.[23]

There's also the sheer pile of money. The United States has the largest nominal gross domestic product (GDP).[24] In GDP based on purchasing power parity (PPP), however, the United States trails China and the European Union.[25] (PPP is a means of calculating exchange rates between currencies that controls for variations in cost of living and pricing.) In neither measure of wealth is the United States a leader per capita.[26] And, even if it were, that wouldn't mean what it sounds like for most people in the United States, because this country with the biggest bucket of cash also has it distributed the most unequally of any wealthy nation, giving the United States both the biggest collection of billionaires[27] on earth and the highest or nearly highest rates of poverty and child-poverty among wealthy nations.[28] The United States ranks 111th out of 150 countries for income equality, according to the CIA[29], or 100th out of 158, according to the World Bank[30], while for equitable distribution of wealth (a very different measure from income), according to one calculation[31], the United States ranks 147th out of 152 countries.

In December 2017, the United Nations Special Rapporteur on Extreme Poverty issued a report on the United States that included these lines:[32]

- US infant mortality rates in 2013 were the highest in the developed world.

- Americans can expect to live shorter and sicker lives, compared to people living in any other rich democracy, and the "health gap" between the US and its peer countries continues to grow.

- US inequality levels are far higher than those in most European countries.

- Neglected tropical diseases, including Zika, are increasingly common in the USA. It has been estimated that 12 million Americans live with a neglected parasitic infection. A 2017 report documents the prevalence of hookworm in Lowndes County, Alabama.

- The US has the highest prevalence of obesity in the developed world.

- In terms of access to water and sanitation the US ranks 36th in the world.

- America has the highest incarceration rate in the world, ahead of Turkmenistan, El Salvador, Cuba, Thailand and the Russian Federation. Its rate is nearly five times the OECD average. [OECD means the Organization for Economic Co-operation and Development, an organization that has 35 member countries.]

- The youth poverty rate in the United States is the highest across the OECD with one quarter of youth living in poverty compared to less than 14 percent across the OECD.

- The Stanford Center on Inequality and Poverty ranks the most well-off countries in terms of labor markets, poverty, safety net, wealth inequality, and economic mobility. The US comes in last of the top 10 most well-off countries, and 18th amongst the top 21.

- In the OECD the US ranks 35th out of 37 in terms of poverty and inequality.

- According to the World Income Inequality Database, the US has the highest Gini rate (measuring inequality) of all Western Countries.

- The Stanford Center on Poverty and Inequality characterizes the US as "a clear and constant outlier in the child poverty league." US child poverty rates are the highest amongst the six richest countries – Canada, the United Kingdom, Ireland, Sweden and Norway.

So, perhaps wealth is not the ideal topic to focus on, any more than freedom or education. We could focus on worker productivity except that the long hours with less vacation enjoyed by U.S. workers do not actually make them the most productive, per hour or per year. That honor goes to the workers of Luxembourg, who put in an average of 29 hours a week, but produce the most GDP per hour and per year. Luxembourg is followed by Ireland, Norway, and Belgium in GDP per hour.[33] The Irish work almost as many hours as U.S. workers, making them also more productive per year.

What about opportunity or social mobility? Isn't the "freedom" of the United States in fact bound up with the idea that, while most people are not the wealthiest, any of them could become the wealthiest with enough hard work? In reality, while there are always exceptions, there are less upward mobility and more firmly entrenched economic classes in the United States than in other wealthy countries.[34]

OK, what about innovation, invention, intellectual

creation? Obviously this is an even harder category than others to quantify, but we can try. Patents filed with the U.S. Patent Office now come more from abroad than from within the United States.[35] But among patents filed anywhere on earth, the United States still applies for and receives a larger number than any other single country, staying slightly ahead of both China and Japan, at least in patents granted. Some reports have China filing more applications than the United States in some recent years. But the U.S. lead evaporates when the comparison is either per-capita or per-GDP. In the former case, South Korea, Japan, Switzerland, and Germany jump ahead. In the latter, South Korea, Japan, China, Germany, Switzerland, and France do.[36] When it comes to new industrial designs, the United States is not at the top by any calculation.[37] And of course these numbers do not tell us the actual creative value or societal impact of all these patents, or how the number of patents filed compares to a society's litigiousness. The United States is, in fact, a world leader in number of lawyers per capita[38], possibly trailing only Israel[39] or Greece[40].

I do give the U.S. some credit for its role (along with the roles of others) in developing the internet, the incredible tool that has allowed me to pull together all of the international comparisons found in this book in a matter of a few days of web surfing.

Then there is popular culture. Published lists of the top money-earning films[41] and music[42] contain almost exclusively U.S. productions. And, while the British -- along with the French, Chinese, Spanish, and others -- dominate the lists of best selling books of all time,[43] U.S. books and other cultural products also have a global impact, especially -- of course -- when turned into films. Out of its many categories for comparing nations, *U.S. News and World Report* ranks the United States first in only one thing: most influential.[44] A U.S.-based ranking of nations' "soft power" places the United States in the top 10.[45] One has to wonder what the world would be like if the countries that were the best at something were also the most influential in regards to the same.

U.S. film distribution, while not strictly limited by

language, also benefits from and contributes to the fact that English is, for largely historical reasons beginning with British imperialism, the third most common first language and first most common second language on earth.[46] The prevalence of English, combined with the size of the United States, likely contributes to the relatively low knowledge of any foreign languages by U.S. adults.[47] And that state of affairs likely contributes to and is further encouraged by the sense of exceptionalism discussed in this book.

Much of the popularity of U.S. films is almost certainly due to the super-expensive high- production quality of those films. But it's reasonable to assume that part of the popularity also stems from the affection many people have in various parts of the world for the stories presented in those films. That people view U.S. movies is, in fact, a common argument for the relative merits of the United States: if it weren't a preferable place, then why do people watch its movies, wear its t-shirts, and try to immigrate to live here?

The United States, it is claimed, accepts more immigrants than any other country. That's actually true,[48] though it's not even close to true on a per-capita or a per-square-mile or a per-GDP basis.[49] It's also not close to true when talking about refugees,[50] only when talking about all types of immigrants combined. U.S. immigration policies favor those with job skills and those from Europe.[51] The United States is also not ranked anywhere near the top of nations that are helpful to immigrants once they arrive, not even according to U.S. studies.[52]

Still, a great many people are willing to abandon their former lives and start anew in the United States, both with legal permission and at risk of legal apprehension. Why? One reason is that, while the average life in the United States, as we will see below, is not the longest, happiest, or healthiest on earth, it's very far from the shortest, most miserable, or most dangerous. The United States may not have Finland's schools or France's paid vacations or Germany's clean energy, but most of its neighborhoods are safer than many places south of its border, for example.

This fact is not, of course, in conflict with the fact that the U.S. government has, in many cases, contributed to the misery from which people who come to the United States are fleeing.[53] That the U.S. government has supported a military coup or trained and armed brutal death squads in a country can be condemned,[54] even while urging that the people fleeing that country be admitted to a chance of a better life in the United States. Neither opposing U.S. militarism nor urging that immigrants be welcomed makes the United States 100 percent Evil or 100 percent Good.

At some point, the attempts to declare the United States Number One in some desirable category take on a quality of desperation. I would so characterize claims of global environmental leadership and claims of global generosity. Let's look at these two concepts, one at a time.

A columnist listing things the United States is #1 in has included marine protected areas and CO_2 emissions reductions.[55] Regarding marine protected areas, the claim turns out to be that the U.S. has the largest area protected under any of six types of protection ranging from strictly protected to "sustainably used." It is a claim not made on a per-square-mile basis.

If it is true that the United States has reduced CO_2 emissions, it certainly needed to, because the United States still trails, at most, only China in this climate-destroying pollution, even considering Europe as one whole; and in CO_2 emissions per capita the United States trails only six countries: Qatar, Kuwait, United Arab Emirates, Oman, Turkmenistan, and Australia.[56] In fact, the U.S. military alone, if it were a country, would rank high on the list of the world's countries for CO_2 emissions.[57] The comparisons are similar for methane and other greenhouse gases. Another study ranks the United States first in CO_2 emissions, first in fertilizer use, second in water pollution, third in marine captures, ninth in species threatened, and second overall (behind Brazil) in environmental destruction[58], although the same study ranks the United States only 55th most destructive out of 179 countries when the level of destruction is adjusted in proportion to the resources each country has available.[59] The British-based Happy Planet Index ranks the United States 137th best out of 140 (only three countries are worse) for ecological footprint.[60]

Meanwhile, the U.S.-based Environmental Performance Index ranks the U.S. 27th best out of 180 countries.[61] However, this is a calculation that emphasizes the current quality of the environment within the United States, not the impact of the United States on the future of the entire planet. It is also a study that rewards the presence of laws, such as those protecting species, rather than focusing on the number of species threatened.

It's worth noting that most environmental studies look at nations' impacts on the world from within their nations' borders, and for most nations that makes perfect sense. However, the U.S. military is a major global force for environmental destruction, with major bases in some 80 countries and with wars in several countries at any given time. The U.S. military is exempt from the Kyoto Treaty[62] and would not be exempt from the Paris Climate Agreement[63] had the U.S. not (uniquely in the world) withdrawn from that treaty, which has been signed by 197, ratified by 175, and is maintained by 174 nations.[64]

A final attempt at a gold medal in world performance is the claim that the United States leads the world in generous giving to the rest of humanity. The claim is sometimes based on government foreign aid and sometimes on private foreign charity, so let's look at both. The latter claim turns out to be the stronger one.

It is routinely claimed that the U.S. government gives the most aid to the world of any government on earth, though less than Europe as a single whole.[65] If this were true, it would not be anywhere close to true as a percentage of gross national income[66] or even per capita.[67] But it isn't true, because unlike other countries, the United States counts as 40 percent of its so-called aid, weapons for foreign militaries. Its biggest recipient of this "security aid" and of overall aid last year was Afghanistan, where the United States is fighting a war. Next was Israel, a wealthy nation to which the United States has given billions of dollars for weapons every year for many years. Third was Egypt. Fourth was Iraq, where the United States is fighting a war.[68] In fact U.S. foreign aid, as a whole, seems to be directed largely around its military policies rather than the relative needs of people in various corners of the earth.

Using U.S. government figures for both private and public giving (including for weapons), one author finds the U.S. still ranked only 15th in foreign generosity as a percentage of income.[69]

However, U.S. private giving abroad is also studied by the U.S.-based Hudson Institute,[70] which identifies dramatically more such giving than numerous other studies.[71] Hudson Institute finds $43.9 billion per year in 2013-2014 from private U.S. donations going abroad. This is, of course, regardless of the quality or efficiency of the charities given to. It is also the highest estimate I've found. Still, if it is accurate, it is indeed an indication of remarkable charitable giving, and without a doubt of remarkable good intentions, regardless of the effectiveness. It is also, if accurate, a real Number 1, even per capita and per GDP.

The Hudson Institute authors go on to add to their calculations for U.S. foreign aid, $108.7 billion in "remittances," that is money sent home by migrants living and working in the United States. To that they add $179.3 billion in "private capital flow" to "developing nations," with no mention of profits or resource extraction or debt payments or any "flow" in the opposite direction. Whether you want to include such figures as measures of U.S. generosity I leave to your discretion.

The above question should not be confused by studies of generosity in general. While the World Giving Index claims that the United States is the second most generous country on earth (after Myanmar),[72] only a tiny fraction of what it looks at is foreign aid,[73] most of it is domestic, and a lot of it is for such projects as funding churches. In fact, about a third of U.S. charity goes to religious organizations, and the next biggest recipients are educational institutions, including universities the donors hope their kids will be admitted to. At most a third of U.S. charity helps the poor in any way, and less than 5 percent goes to help the poor outside of the United States. On balance, the tax deduction for charitable giving in the United States appears to enrich the rich.[74] Nonetheless, for better or worse, and regardless of how exactly it can be compared to very different societies, charity is very big business in the United States, and there is certainly something positive in that fact that should be encouraged and should give us hope as we progress through the more negative information that lies ahead.

As we have reviewed claims for first place, we have seen that very few pan out and that most are false, either across the board or when put into perspective by population or geography or wealth. I have tried to include all of the major claims commonly made. I have left out such claims to glory as most cheese, most cats, most dogs, and most rollercoasters, not because of any prejudice against such things, but because they seem less significant, less cross-cultural, and almost infinitely expandable. It is my contention that most people who wave U.S. flags and shout "we're number one!" do not have in mind statistics on cheese or corn dog production. I have also excluded from the preceding discussion those claims to fame that I actually consider points of shame rather than pride, such as most expensive military, most foreign military bases, most square miles paved with asphalt, most television viewing, etc., all of which will be listed below. I will explain why I consider each category a negative, rather than a positive, and the reader can make his or her own judgment.

FAIR TO MIDDLING

First, however, I want to turn to some of the many other categories in which the United States does horribly in comparison with other wealthy countries but still pretty well in comparison with poor countries. Let's call these the fair to middling categories. Some of those items already discussed above, as we have seen, actually belong here too.

Let's start with a few of the features that I think it would be most important for a nation to excel at in order to claim a general superiority: life expectancy, health, and happiness.

The United States comes in 31st for life expectancy out of 183 countries according to the World Health Organization (WHO),[75] 43rd out of 201 according to the United Nations,[76] 43rd out of 223 according to the CIA,[77] or tied for 26th out of 34 according to the Organization for Economic Co-operation and Development (OECD).[78] People in the United States can expect, on average, to live longer than in most countries on earth, but not as long as in most other wealthy countries. Using the WHO numbers, of the 30 countries where life expectancy is longer than in the United States, 25 of them have a lower GDP per capita. Costa Rica, with a higher life expectancy, has less than 20 percent the GDP per capita of the

United States. Of six nations with higher GDP per capita, only Qatar has lower life expectancy.

The U.S. health problem undoubtedly has many factors, but the healthcare factor is not a problem of failing to spend money. The United States spends more per capita on healthcare than any other nation.[79] But it spends it inefficiently,[80] and its steadfast refusal to borrow health coverage ideas from other nations is an example of the damaging effects of exceptionalism that we will be looking at below. One key way in which the United States spends inefficiently is by not providing coverage for millions of people. Uniquely among wealthy nations, the United States does not provide health coverage as a universal right, but treats it as a privilege that some cannot afford, resulting in great suffering and great bureaucracy.[81] The World Economic Forum ranks the United States 29th in health.[82]

The U.S.-based organization Save the Children ranks the United States the 33rd best place to be a mother and raise children.[83] The CIA ranks the United States

56th best in preventing infant mortality.[84] Among world capitals in wealthy countries, Washington D.C. ranks worst for infant mortality.[85] A U.S.-based study of the 20 wealthiest countries found the U.S. worst for child mortality.[86] The United Nations Children's Fund (UNICEF) ranks the United States 26th out of 29 wealthy countries for overall wellbeing of children.[87] Alone among 41 wealthy countries, the United States does not provide paid parental leave for all workers.[88]

Contributing to U.S. shortcomings in life expectancy and health is its leadership in violence. The U.S.-based National Academies of Sciences, Engineering, and Medicine looked at 17 wealthy countries and found the U.S. such a leader in violent deaths that it reached almost three times the violent death rate of the second-place nation.[89] By UN figures, the U.S. murder rate is worse than in 125 countries and better than in 93 countries.[90] A study by the U.S.-based *American Journal of Medicine* of 23 populous, high-income nations[91] found that,

US homicide rates were 7.0 times higher than in other high-income countries, driven by a gun homicide rate that was 25.2 times higher. For 15- to 24-year-olds, the gun homicide rate in the United States was 49.0 times higher. Firearm-related suicide rates were 8.0 times higher in the United States, but the overall suicide rates were average. Unintentional firearm deaths were 6.2 times higher in the United States. The overall firearm death rate in the United States from all causes was 10.0 times higher. Ninety percent of women, 91 percent of children aged 0 to 14 years, 92 percent of youth aged 15 to 24 years, and 82 percent of all people killed by firearms were from the United States.

You may want to stand up, and jump around, and not sit down for this next one. A study published by the *Lancet* found that 75 countries had a smaller percentage of inactive adults than in the United States, while 44 countries had more of their adults inactive (getting very little exercise).[92] A study of 29 nations found that in only 9 of them did people, on average, spend fewer minutes on exercise than in the United States.[93]

Meanwhile, rankings for obesity place the United States anywhere from first[94] to 12th[95] to 18th[96] to 19th[97] to 27th[98] out of the world's nations for the prevalence of obesity in its population. Primarily Pacific island nations and some nations in the Middle East tend to be ranked ahead of the United States on this one. Some 200 other nations have less obesity than the United States.

So much for health and life. And we've previously looked at liberty. What about the pursuit (and attainment) of happiness? The UN-initiated, U.S.-, France-, and India-based World Happiness Report ranks the United States 14th in happiness out of 155 countries.[99] The British-based Happy Planet Index, which looks at wellbeing, life expectancy, inequality, and ecological footprint, ranks the United States 108th out of 140.[100]

The UN's Human Development Index, which considers life expectancy, expected and mean years of schooling, gross national income (GNI), and GNI per capita, ranks the United States 10th, tied with Canada, and trailing the usual suspects from Northern Europe plus Singapore.[101]

The British-based Good Country Index, which looks at science and technology, culture, international peace and security, world order, planet and climate, prosperity and equality, and health and well being, is certainly not something I entirely agree with in terms of its priorities and values. But many people agree with much of it, and it ranks the United States no higher than 10th in any category, and 25th overall out of 163 countries.[102]

Another key consideration might be all the things lumped under the heading of infrastructure. The Swiss-based World Economic Forum's Global Competitiveness Index ranks the United States 25th in "basic requirements" including ninth in "infrastructure" (though it does put the U.S. first in "efficiency enhancers").[103] Looking more specifically at the percentage of electricity in each country generated by renewable resources, the United States comes in at 124th place.[104]

A central concern, both in my mind and in the common conception of the merits of the United States, is that of democracy -- by which I mean majority, popular, or consensus rule. So, which countries are actually the most democratic? As noted in the discussion of freedom above, the British-based *Economist Magazine*'s Democracy Index puts the United States in a three-way tie for 20th place.[105] This index claims to look at "electoral process and pluralism," "civil liberties," the "functioning of government," "political participation," and "political culture." It identifies 19 "full democracies" and places the United States among the "flawed democracies," albeit at the very top of that group.

But let's get more specific. Actual democracy means popular decision making. In some countries, including the United States, there may be more such democracy at the local or regional level, as there probably should be. But the U.S. national government dominates U.S. policy making, so it's reasonable, as well as feasible, for us to compare national governments.

When it comes to the use of referenda to set national policy, Switzerland leads the way, followed by Italy.[106] But, of course, "democracy" most often actually refers to government by representatives who act on the basis of public opinion. So, which nations have the best representative republics? This could be investigated in endless depth and complexity, including by considering the number of constituents per representative, whether it's easy for citizens to vote, whether elections are winner-take-all or proportional, whether ranked-choice voting is used, whether a less-representative body can overrule a more-representative one, etc. The United States would be unlikely to fare well in most such analyses.

One clearer comparison that cuts across much of this detail is the question of the financial cost of getting elected. In some nations, more of the money is recorded and duly tallied. In some it is more often silently slipped under the table. In some places we disdainfully speak of bribery and in others respectfully talk of "campaign contributions" (charitable people that we are). But when it comes to the bottom line, there is little doubt that no other country comes close to the U.S. level of financial corruption of elections.[107]

Money isn't the only problem with U.S. elections. There are hurdles in the way of registering and of voting, long lines, malfunctioning and unverifiable machines, poor and unfair media coverage, names incorrectly stripped from voter rolls, obstacles to entering races and getting into debates and into the media, and many other factors. The Australian-based Election Integrity Project ranks the United States at the bottom of a list of 23 "democracies" from around the world.[108]

Regardless of what you think of U.S. "democracy," the people who live in the United States think less of it than people in other countries think of theirs, as measured by the very minimal participation of voting. The U.S.-based Pew Research Center found that a smaller percentage of the voting-age public in the United States votes than in 13 out of 18 countries examined.[109]

In the end, there is one true test of democracy, and that is whether public policies are determined by public opinion. In the United States they are not. Researchers at Princeton and Northwestern University have found the United States to be an oligarchy in which the wealthy elite largely determines government policy -- which lines up with popular opinion only when popular and elite opinion agree.[110] I haven't found a similar study comparing the world's nations, though I strongly suspect that the United States is not the only one most commonly called "democracy" and most accurately called "oligarchy." The point is that not only are there other nations more democratic than the United States, but the United States doesn't even enter into that competition at all. In fact it is hard to find a U.S. politician who doesn't proclaim his or her independence by proudly claiming to ignore, rather than to follow, public opinion polls. (Another measure: the United States may rank first, possibly even ahead of the British, in obsession with the British royalty.)[111]

Related to the question of democracy is that of promoting or spreading democracy, as a beneficial service to the rest of the world. Nations that do this through leading by example also do it in a manner compatible with democratic tendencies. While "spreading democracy" is a common element in war propaganda, it is not clear that warmaking has actually helped in this regard. In fact, just the opposite may be the case. The United States has, in recent years, provided military aid to 73 percent of the world's dictatorships, and military training to many of them.[112] The U.S. government, since World War II, has overthrown at least 36 governments, interfered in at least 84 foreign elections, attempted to assassinate over 50 foreign leaders, and dropped bombs on people in over 30 countries.[113] Many of the nations on the receiving end of these efforts were democracies.

In February 2018, *New York Times* reporter Scott Shane wrote:

> [According to two authorities, in recent decades] Russian and American interferences in elections have not been morally equivalent. American interventions have generally been aimed at helping non-authoritarian candidates challenge dictators or otherwise promoting democracy. Russia has more often intervened to disrupt democracy or promote authoritarian rule, they said.[114]

The very same article in which Shane quotes this claim includes a link to a scholarly report[115] that cites numerous recent cases of U.S. interference in elections within nations generally counted as democracies.[116] Also in February 2018, former CIA director James Woolsey was interviewed on Fox News:[117]

LAURA INGRAHAM: Have we ever tried to meddle in other countries' elections?

JAMES WOOLSEY: Oh, probably. But it was for the good of the system, in order to avoid the communists from taking over.

LAURA INGRAHAM: Yeah.

JAMES WOOLSEY: For example, in Europe in '47, '48, '49, the Greeks and the Italians, we—CIA—

LAURA INGRAHAM: We don't do that now, though? We don't mess around in other people's elections, Jim?

JAMES WOOLSEY: Well, mmm, yum, yum, yum, never mind. Only for a very good cause.

LAURA INGRAHAM: Can you do that—let's do a vine video and—as former CIA director. I love it.

JAMES WOOLSEY: Only for very good cause—

LAURA INGRAHAM: OK.

JAMES WOOLSEY: —in the interests of democracy.

The United States also partners in wars with allies like Saudi Arabia that are among the least democratic on earth. The U.S. military may, in fact, be one of the greatest impediments to democracy in existence, which brings us to the subject of undesirable gold medals.

OH NO, NOT NUMBER ONE!

If you identify with the United States, you may want to jump ahead and read my advice against identifying with any nation, and then come back and read this next section. This is where we look at areas in which the United States is indeed ranked first but shouldn't want to be. Some of these areas have already been mentioned above, but let's start with the biggest ones.

Where the United States most dramatically stands apart from the rest of the world is in a general area on which a lot of U.S. films also tend to focus: war and "crime fighting" -- or, more specifically, militarism and incarceration.

In military spending, the U.S. government has no peer. Using numbers from the Stockholm International Peace Research Institute (SIPRI), the United States spent $611 billion in 2016, almost three times the next nearest nation, and significantly more than the next nearest eight nations combined, six of which are U.S. allies that the U.S. State Department pushes to spend more.[118] And U.S. military spending soared in 2017 and 2018, with the U.S. President proposing $727 billion for 2019.[119] In addition, careful analysts have found that beyond the Pentagon budget, a full count of U.S. military spending should include the nuclear weapons in the Department of Energy, and the war activities of the State Department, Homeland Security Department, and numerous other agencies, including the secretive war spying agencies. That adds another $200 billion or so. A maximally inclusive military budget would also take count of spending on veterans and on the debt for past military spending. That adds yet another $400 billion or so, taking the total well over $1,200 billion per year.[120] Only 19 other nations on earth spend more than $10 billion per year. Seventeen of them are U.S. allies and weapons customers.

When military spending is considered per capita, using SIPRI numbers, the top nations are all U.S. allies.[121] But the fourth, fifteenth, and twenty-first overall spenders (Saudi Arabia, Israel, and Singapore) jump ahead of the United States. (SIPRI includes no numbers for North Korea.) One of these nations, Israel, only achieves its position by virtue of billions of dollars for military spending that the United States gives to it as a present each year; whether you want to count that as Israeli or U.S. military spending is up to you. If such U.S. spending on Israel, Egypt, and other nations were added to the U.S. account, the United States might surpass Singapore as well as Israel in per capita military spending, but nothing any accountant could do would put any nation anywhere near Saudi Arabia. Both Saudi Arabia and Singapore are U.S. allies and weapons customers -- Saudi Arabia its largest weapons customer and its partner in the current war on Yemen. There's also a way in which the per capita comparison makes the U.S. spending appear even larger than a straightforward comparison, namely what a per capita comparison does to the world's second and third biggest overall spenders, China and Russia. On a per capita basis China and Russia drop off the list of top military spenders, leaving only the United States and its chosen allies.

But the impact of a massive military is first and foremost on the rest of the earth, not on the nation that pays for it. And its creation is principally the action of an oligarchy, not a populace. So, while the per capita comparison is useful, the absolute investment remains, as we will see, enormously significant.

It's popular, including among boosters of military spending, to rank military spending in proportion to each nation's wealth or GDP. The reason should be obvious. If other nations are spending a tiny fraction of what yours spends on militarism, that hardly encourages the purchase of more expensive weaponry. But if those nations have small economies and are spending a higher percentage of their money on their puny militaries, the United States can more easily be persuaded to spend-spend-spend to try to close the percentage-of-GDP gap! Based on the same SIPRI numbers, which still do not include North Korea, 10 nations outpace the United States in military spending per dollar of GDP.[122] Nine of them are U.S. allies and weapons customers. Six of them spend less than 2 percent what the United States does. One is Russia, which spends about 10 percent of what the United States does, according to SIPRI. (Incidentally, Iran spends about 2 percent what the United States does, and North Korea -- even by the most extravagant estimates -- about 0.5 percent.)

U.S. military spending is notoriously wasteful and unaccountable, but so is much of the rest of the world's military spending. So how do dollars translate into actual militaries? Well, here's a list of the top employers in the world:[123]

1. The U.S. military.
2. The Chinese military.
3. Wal-Mart.
4. McDonald's.

In this case, "U.S. military," means the Department of Defense, not even counting personnel in all of those other U.S. government departments that have military spending.

All non-U.S. nations combined have fewer than 30 military bases outside of their own territory, while the United States has at least 800.[124] The creation of quite a few of these bases has involved the eviction of the local populations. These include bases in Diego Garcia, Greenland, Alaska, Hawaii, Panama, Puerto Rico, the Marshall Islands, Guam, the Philippines, Okinawa, and South Korea.[125]

Many U.S. bases are hosted by brutal dictatorships, which returns us to the topic of "spreading democracy." An academic study has identified a strong U.S. tendency to defend dictatorships where the United States has bases. [126] A glance at a newspaper will tell you the same. Crimes in Bahrain (major base) are not equal to crimes in Iran (no bases). In fact, when brutal and undemocratic governments currently hosting U.S. bases (in, for example, Honduras, Aruba, Curaçao, Mauritania, Liberia, Niger, Burkina Faso, Central African Republic, Chad, Egypt, Mozambique, Burundi, Kenya, Uganda, Ethiopia, Djibouti, Yemen, Qatar, Oman, UAE, Bahrain, Saudi Arabia, Kuwait, Jordan, Israel, Turkey, Georgia, Afghanistan, Pakistan, Thailand, Cambodia, or Singapore) are protested, there is a pattern of increased U.S. support for those governments, which makes eviction of the U.S. bases all the more likely should the government fall, which fuels a vicious cycle that increases popular resentment of the U.S. government. The U.S. began building new bases in Honduras shortly after the 2009 coup.

The world's biggest military budget doesn't produce an undisputed lead only in military personnel and foreign bases, but also in aircraft carriers, cruisers, destroyers, nuclear submarines, military aircraft, etc.[127] The vast majority of the world's nuclear weapons are in the arsenals of Russia and the United States, with the United States investing major new funds in that area.

Contrary to the notion that preparing for war prevents wars, increased military spending has tended to result in more wars -- with the United States, by far, leading the world in the number of wars it takes part in, the nations in bombs, and the nations it strikes with missiles from drones. In recent years, the United States has engaged in serious bombing campaigns in Afghanistan, Iraq, Pakistan, Syria, Libya, Somalia, and Yemen, and numerous smaller operations in many other countries. While NATO and other allies have assisted the United States in some of these wars, no other countries have done anything remotely like this level of war fighting far from their own borders. The closest parallel is Russian participation in a single war in Syria.[128]

Most of the nations where wars are fought do not manufacture weapons of war. Most weapons of war come from a handful of nations, led by the United States,[129] resulting in numerous wars having U.S.-made weapons on more than one side of the war. In some cases, such as Syria, we've even seen U.S. armed and trained troops fighting each other.[130]

I promised that I would explain why I think some claims to first place in the world are points of shame rather than pride. In very brief, and as elaborated on the website WorldBeyondWar.org and in some of my previous books, war is counterproductive on its own terms, generating more enemies than it kills. While making us less safe[131] in the name of protecting our "freedom," war strips away our liberties.[132] Recent wars have brought us warrantless surveillance, drone attacks, imprisonment without charge, and all kinds of restrictions on speech and assembly. Militarism is the top destroyer of the natural environment[133], top drain on wealth[134], and a trade-off that one cannot morally make when fractions of military spending could save and improve many more lives than war damages. The United Nations calculates that $30 billion per year could end starvation on earth, and $11 billion end the lack of clean drinking water.[135] Go back and read the dollar figures for the U.S. military budget.

One of the results of U.S. militarism is the militarization of U.S. culture. As the only nation on earth that has not ratified the Convention on the Rights of the Child[136] (which is not to suggest that all ratifiers fully comply with it) the U.S. military runs programs like the Junior Reserve Officer Training Corps (JROTC) that train students to shoot guns in their schools. One such student engaged in the mass-murder of his fellow students in a Florida high school, just weeks before I wrote this book.[137] The U.S. military also unloads its old weapons on local police departments and the general public, and engages in training local police departments. The rate of gun ownership per capita in the United States is an undisputed first place in the world, surpassing rich and poor nations, nations at peace, and nations at war.[138] The closest competitor, Serbia, has about half as many guns per capita as the United States. One common justification for stockpiling guns in the United States is to supposedly fight off the U.S. government, the same government whose flag and anthem have acquired a status of holiness.

We've already mentioned violent deaths in the United States. One type is death by police, a category in which the United States absolutely dwarfs other wealthy nations,[139] while trailing some poor nations.[140] Another is death by state execution. In this category, the United States has fallen to seventh place among the 23 nations that are on the list at all, trailing behind China, Iran, Saudi Arabia, Iraq, Pakistan, and Egypt.[141] If drone strikes that U.S. presidents talk about as executions were included, the United States would jump into an easy lead.

Where the United States truly excels is not in executing prisoners, but in packing them into prisons and keeping them there. The "land of the free" leads the world in prisoners, both overall and by a per capita comparison (with the possible exception, on a per capita basis, of the Seychelles).[142] The United States really does have less than 5 percent of the world's people and almost 25 percent of the world's prisoners. The United States is also an outlier in its practice -- again in violation of the Convention on the Rights of the Child -- of putting minors in prison for life with no possibility of parole, as well as in its use of solitary confinement.[143] In comparison with the prisons of other wealthy nations, U.S. prisons are notoriously brutal and often directed toward anything but rehabilitation. While the U.S. government is exporting prison-construction and increased incarceration to other countries, none of those others has begun to challenge the United States in the rankings.[144] The U.S. lead in incarceration has not always existed and need not exist forever. I'd prefer to see it disappear by decarceration in the United States, rather than by greater incarceration elsewhere.

Beyond militarism and incarceration, the walk of shame takes the United States past some categories already touched on above: a possible (non-per-capita) first place in CO_2 emissions and first in fertilizer use,[145] a possible first in obesity per capita,[146] a possible first in lawyers per capita[147] (Sorry! Don't sue me!), a first in billionaires[148] (I don't apologize for finding that undesirable -- any billionaire who reads this is welcome to share his/her wealth and cease to be one at any moment), and a resounding first in student debt overall and per capita and in amount of debt per indebted student.[149]

There are a number of what I consider undesirable firsts that the United States holds that we have not yet examined: television viewing per capita,[150] square miles paved with asphalt (beaten out by India when compared per total square miles of land),[151] road motor vehicles per capita (unless you count San Marino or Monaco),[152] wasted food per capita (a U.S.-based organization finds 40 percent of food wasted in the United States[153] and the UN reports that North America leads the world in wasting food[154]), cosmetic surgeries overall and probably per capita,[155] and nobody else even close in pornography production.[156]

The United States, among the world's nations, is only third worst in depression, anxiety, and alcohol and drug use, so that's something.[157]

DIVISIONS WITHIN THE UNITED STATES

Before leaving the topic of how the United States compares with other countries, we should look briefly at some unique elements in U.S. culture, including the status in the United States of racism, sexism, and LGBT rights, and the religiosity and puritanism that in some ways align the United States with some of the poorer countries of the earth, with which it is also aligned in so many of the categories we have already examined.

Is the United States a model of post-racial multi-ethnic inclusivity, or a bastion of the most entrenched bigotry? I think, pretty clearly, it is both. While the United States grew out of genocide and slavery, with long traditions of bigotry, many in the United States have made outstanding progress toward better thoughts and practices. Still, the resistance to socialism -- and to social-democratic reforms -- that has created so many low rankings for the United States in quality of life among wealthy nations has been facilitated by racist attitudes and myths. So has the acceptance of mass incarceration and police killings. So has the expansion of wars and drone killings. Racist habits are both more entrenched and better understood and overcome in the United States than in some other countries.

The United States is also of two minds when it comes to women's rights, with feminism having made great strides, but with a culture of violent masculinity pushing back. The United States has never passed an Equal Rights Amendment, and is the only Western "democracy" not to have ratified the Convention on the Elimination of All Forms of Discrimination Against Women.[158] Save the Children ranks the United States 32nd in opportunities for girls,[159] in part because of a high rate of teen pregnancies -- which can be attributed to a culture that celebrates personal independence, enjoyment, freedom, and sexuality, but also represses sex and does a poor job of sex education.

The United States has rapidly come a long ways toward equal rights for LGBTQ people, but by various measures lags behind some other Western nations.[160] During the George W. Bush presidency, the United States allied with authoritarian Islamic states to oppose reproductive and gay rights at the United Nations, going against the position of most Western nations and of the later Obama administration.

The United States stands out among wealthy countries, and resembles more impoverished countries, in its level of religiosity,[161] and in the puritanical and fundamentalist traditions of much of that religiosity -- and, as we will see, of some of the origins of exceptionalist thinking. In his 2017 book, *Exceptional America*, Mugambi Jouet makes a case that religion in the United States contributes to authoritarian thinking and to a uniquely American sort of anti-intellectualism. The United States is the only Western nation with a large portion of the population believing in creationism,[162] not to mention angels, the devil, and hell. President George W. Bush revealed that God had instructed him to launch wars, and shortly before I sat down to write this book Oprah Winfrey announced that she would run for U.S. president if God told her to.[163]

It seems possible to me that one contributing factor in the U.S. public's anxiety in recent years over "fake news" and foreign propaganda is the desire to identify a proper authority who will reveal the truth, rather than the desire to seek out and test competing claims in a complex world.

Of course that describes only one section of the U.S. public, and in all of these matters, when I say the United States is of two minds, I am using a metaphor. A nation has no mind. Some people are of one mind and some of another, and perhaps certain people are themselves conflicted -- we all often are. But, as we will see below, there is widespread agreement, as on little else, on the practice of exceptionalist thinking.

WHERE WOULD A WISE BABY MOST WANT TO BE BORN?

By this point in this book, if nothing else, we should be rid of the false belief that the best place to live in the world is necessarily anywhere in the United States. In many of the quality of life criteria that I've looked at, in which the United States finished 30th or 120th, the same handful of nations finished at the top: Norway, Denmark, Sweden, Iceland, Finland, Netherlands, Switzerland, Costa Rica. I do not recommend emigrating. (Nor do I oppose it.) I do not recommend taking pride in some new nation or feeling shame about some old nation. Not only does quality of life vary by region and small community, but the best place for one person is not the best place for another. Ties to family and friends and land are often of more value in an individual life than an improvement in national infrastructure. Nations that have shortcomings have the most need precisely of those who recognize the shortcomings and want to make improvements. What I recommend is ceasing to identify with any national government, and ceasing to believe that doing so makes you superior to anyone else.

II. Exceptionalist Thinking

Now, a burning question ought to be how exactly the above mediocre-to-miserable results of comparing the United States with the rest of the world justify such an incredible quantity of U.S. flags on display, or the first place achieved by the United States in polls measuring national pride,[164] or the widespread belief within the United States in its superiority to everywhere else.[165] Some small part of the answer may be that the United States used to compare better in some ways, and old habits of thought that flatter the thinker die hard. But the biggest part of the answer, I think, is that exceptionalism is not based on factual observations at all.

IT'S EXCEPTIONAL NOT TO BE AN EXCEPTIONALIST

Views of at least some portion of the U.S. public stand apart from those of other nations. In a study of 20 wealthy so-called democracies in Europe, Canada, Australia, New Zealand, Japan, and the

United States, the U.S. public was the most inclined to blame the poor for poverty, believed the most in myths of meritocracy, was the most religious, was the most believing by far in the existence of "Hell," was the most proud of its nationality, was the most supportive of attacking other countries (or using "pre-emptive force"), was the most supportive of attacking other countries without the U.N.'s blessing, and was the next to the worst in homophobia.[166] The U.S. public also registers as the most opposed to "strong government," even while remaining oddly oblivious to and supportive of the world's most powerful government in the areas of war, weapons dealing, assassination, imprisonment, mass surveillance, etc.

In 1995-96 and 2003-04 pollsters surveyed people in over 20 countries on how they ranked their countries in general and in various areas of accomplishment. Both in terms of general pride in the United States and in terms of various specifics, the people of the United States ranked second in the earlier study and first in the later one in level of national pride.[167]

On some of these points, there is a sharp divide between two parts of the U.S. public, with some U.S. residents having more in common with other nations' publics than with the U.S. right wing. On other questions there is less division, and beliefs that would be extreme elsewhere are large-majority views in the United States. Among the latter, is the U.S. belief in national exceptionalism (even among those who haven't heard of the term).

Exceptionalism is anachronistically fact-based to the extent that it is based on states of affairs that used to exist. In Alexis de Tocqueville's time, the U.S. did allow a relatively high percentage of its public to vote. It did have greater freedom of press. It did have greater equality of wealth than did Western Europe. It did have desirable job openings for which higher education was no benefit whatsoever, yet it was creating the most educated public around. None of those things bears any connection to current reality.

The biggest component of exceptionalism seems completely unrelated to facts. The belief in a divine mission is an attitude, not an observation. Hilde Eliassen Restad suggested in *Newsweek* in 2016 that "Americans have, throughout their history, believed they are a superior people, believed they are endowed with a unique mission, believed that they will never succumb to the merciless laws of history. Most importantly, it's an idea that Americans and their leaders have often acted upon in the world."[168]

In 2010, 80 percent of those polled by Gallup in the United States said the United States had a unique character that made it the greatest country in the world. But only 58 percent said they believed that then-President Barack Obama shared their belief in U.S. exceptionalism.[169] Part of the reason for that low result might be that Obama had said this in 2009: "I believe in American exceptionalism, just as I suspect that the Brits believe in British exceptionalism and the Greeks believe in Greek exceptionalism."[170] That, of course, is a statement of utter disbelief in American exceptionalism. To state that you view the United States as others view their own other countries is to make your view unexceptional, if not to suggest an understanding of it as a provincial delusion. Obama was later compelled to correct his heresy: "I believe in American exceptionalism with every fiber of my being." While numerous Republican politicians accused Obama of lacking a belief in exceptionalism, Hillary Clinton made the same accusation against Donald Trump.[171]

Poll results are very dependent on the exact language used. "Greatest country in the world" is a vague phrase used so frequently as to almost go unheard or to count as a truism, almost part of the name of the United States. Yet when Pew in 2011 gave people options of "greatest country" or "one of the greatest countries," 48 percent picked the former and 42 percent the latter. And when Pew asks U.S. residents if they agree with this statement: "Our people are not perfect, but our culture is superior to others," the pollsters are close to demanding hard-corps snobs and bigots willing to proclaim their superiority to 96 percent of humanity. So they do not get 80 percent or 90 percent agreeing. But they did get 60 percent in 2002, 55 percent in 2007, and 49 percent in 2011. This claim to superiority seems to be on a downward trend, especially as young people polled were less supportive of it than old people.[172]

A 2013 survey of 1,000 U.S. adults found that 49 percent had not heard of American Exceptionalism. But 72 percent agreed or strongly agreed that the United States is "unique and unlike any other nation," 35 percent that the U.S. is "morally better than most other countries," 28 percent that the U.S. is "free of rigid class distinctions," and 20 percent that the U.S. is "like the biblical shining city upon a hill."[173] That last one being at only 20 percent should give us some hope!

EXCEPTIONALISTS IN THEIR OWN WORDS

From John Winthrop before the fact to Tocqueville and on through John Kennedy and Ronald Reagan, up to and including Barack Obama, Donald Trump, and most voices on U.S. television news today, as well as that neighbor or friend who's never left the United States but assures us it is "the greatest country on earth," a consensus has evolved and solidified around the idea of U.S. exceptionalism. It is the point of agreement between those who would "make America great again" and those who declare it to be "already great." It's an idea that has grown more strident and a bit defensive at the same time. But it's a "belief" in the sense of a religious belief, not an ordinary belief strictly connected to any disagreement with the facts I've laid out above.

For many people in the United States it is commonplace to describe this country as uniquely free, democratic, and capitalist; as the best place to live on earth; and as the one nation indispensable to upholding the rule of law. A careful examination, as we have seen, finds the United States to be indeed unique in a remarkable number of ways, but not always in the ways imagined. In fact, the assumptions and motivations of exceptionalism turn out to be no more factual or benign than those of racism or sexism or other forms of bigotry.

In 2018, millions of Americans believed God had chosen Trump for the presidency.[174] They were squarely in the nonpartisan tradition of exceptionalist thinking. "[T]here can be little question that the hand of providence has been on a nation which finds a Washington, a Lincoln, or a Roosevelt when it needs him," wrote Seymour Martin Lipset in 1995 with an apparently straight face and no hint at whose hand was responsible for, say, Zachary Taylor, William McKinley, or Richard Nixon. Lipset was a past president of both the American Political Science Association and the American Sociological Association and had been elected to the American Philosophical Society, the National Academy of Sciences, and the American Academy of Arts and Sciences. He had taught at Harvard and Stanford. And in his well-received book *American Exceptionalism: A Double-Edged Sword*, from which the above quote is taken, he informed us that America was indeed exceptional, and that the "hand of providence" made it so.[175]

U.S. presidents since Ronald Reagan have rarely given speeches without asking (or telling?) God to bless America. Congress begins each day with

a prayer. Presidents as far apart as McKinley and
Bush the Second have informed us that they never
attacked other countries without receiving God's
direct approval or instruction. During the so-called
French and Indian War, Americans believed the
French to be the forces of the Antichrist, a pattern
that, in some form, has accompanied dozens of
wars since. When President Donald Trump in 2018
declared Jerusalem the capital of Israel, he attended
a rally in Florida at which a state senator applauded
the move on the grounds that it would usher in
Armageddon. The crowd cheered.[176]

In his 2015 book *American Exceptionalism and Civil
Religion*, John D. Wilsey argues that in the absence of
a state religion, the United States has made a religion
of nationalism.[177] National cemeteries and the tomb
of the unknown soldier are holy places. Children
who refuse to pledge allegiance to the flag in school,
and football players who refuse to participate in flag
rituals as the national anthem is sung, may experience
a wide range of unpleasant repercussions. President
Trump asked the National Football League (NFL) to

fire any player guilty of "disrespecting our flag." The U.S. flag appears on Catholic altars in some states, as well as in other churches and sacred arenas. Ft. McHenry in Baltimore is not a historic site. It is a "National Monument and Historic Shrine." For some, the Confederate flag and statues of Confederate generals are equally sacred. But virtually nobody treats local or state (except perhaps Texas) or United Nations or world flags as sacred. It is exclusively the flag that accompanies a military that must be worshiped — a military that pays the NFL and other sports leagues millions of public dollars to perform fly-overs of fighter jets and other pro-military ceremonies.[178]

In President Trump's first State of the Union speech in January 2018, he said:

> In America, we know that faith and family, not government and bureaucracy, are the center of the American life. Our motto is 'in God we trust.' And we celebrate our police, our military, and our amazing veterans as

heroes who deserve our total and unwavering support. Here tonight is Preston Sharp, a 12-year-old boy from Redding, California, who noticed that veterans' graves were not marked with flags on Veterans Day. He decided to change that, and started a movement that has now placed 40,000 flags at the graves of our great heroes. Preston: a job well done. Young patriots like Preston teach all of us about our civic duty as Americans. Preston's reverence for those who have served our Nation reminds us why we salute our flag, why we put our hands on our hearts for the pledge of allegiance, and why we proudly stand for the national anthem.[179]

In much of the world, if you see any flag at all, you can safely ignore it without being suspended from school or shut out of your sports career. In *Exceptional America*, Jouet writes: "In most other democracies, flags hang mainly on government buildings. . . . Anthems are also generally reserved for national holidays or competitions involving national teams. . . . National chauvinism has evolved into a religion in America."[180]

This extreme nationalism is usually not just intense love for home. It generally includes a belief in superiority and a sense of duty to an incredibly arrogant and condescending mission. Abraham Keteltas, Wilsey recounts, a Presbyterian preacher in Newburyport, Massachusetts, in 1777 equated the war against England with the cause of God.[181] From the earliest settlers to believers in Manifest Destiny to President McKinley (who asked God how to govern more distant "little brown" people supposedly unready to govern themselves), exceptionalists have had a mission.

"We Americans," wrote Herman Melville in 1850 in the voice of a fictional character expressing, not Melville's view but a common one, "are the peculiar chosen people -- the Israel of our time; we bear the ark of the liberties of the world. . . . God has predestinated, mankind expects, great things from our race."[182]

On January 22, 2018, U.S. Vice President Mike Pence spoke to the Israeli Knesset: "In the story of the Jews, we've always seen the story of America. It is the story of an exodus, a journey from persecution to freedom, a story that shows the power of faith and the promise of hope. My country's very first settlers also saw themselves as pilgrims, sent by Providence, to build a new Promised Land. The songs and stories of the people of Israel were their anthems, and they faithfully taught them to their children, and do to this day. And our founders, as others have said, turned to the wisdom of the Hebrew Bible for direction, guidance and inspiration."[183]

One of the most attractive ideas promoted as U.S. exceptionalism (and it has indeed been accompanied by actual nice events and behaviors) is that only in the U.S. is citizenship a question of one's choosing to be part of a great democratic experiment, rather than a question of one's ancestry. Supporters of this idea take as proof of it the alleged uniqueness of the term "un-American." Only a national identity that amounts to a way of thinking, they argue, can have a contrary way of being. Since being Canadian is just a mundane legal question, there can be no such thing as doing something un-Canadian, whereas un-American thoughts are perfectly possible, because being American is a question of thinking properly.

But not only is there a great danger in defining improper ways of thinking as depriving the thinker of his or her rights, but charges of un-Americanism have almost always, if not always, been associated with foreign national enemies. And enemies have been identified and demonized because of their ways of thinking, including the top two enemies of recent decades: godless communism and Muslim terrorism. When President Barack Obama was widely accused of lacking faith in American Exceptionalism, he was also accused of being a foreigner and a Muslim.

Dick Cheney's and Liz Cheney's 2015 book, *Exceptional: Why the World Needs a Powerful America*, is in part a partisan tirade that finds zero flaws in the United States other than the cursed existence of the Democratic Party.[184] In a broader sense, it is a portrait of a widely accepted worldview that was also articulated in then-President Barack Obama's 2009 Nobel Peace Prize acceptance speech -- the only such speech in 117 years to have defended war making.

"There will be times," said Obama, "when nations – acting individually or in concert – will find the use of force not only necessary but morally justified. I make this statement mindful of what Martin Luther King Jr. said in this same ceremony years ago: 'Violence never brings permanent peace. It solves no social problem: it merely creates new and more complicated ones.' As someone who stands here as a direct consequence of Dr. King's life work, I am living testimony to the moral force of non-violence. I know there's nothing weak – nothing passive – nothing naïve – in the creed and lives of Gandhi and King. But as a head of state sworn to protect and defend my nation, I cannot be guided by their examples alone. I face the world as it is, and cannot stand idle in the face of threats to the American people. For make no mistake: Evil does exist in the world. A non-violent movement could not have halted Hitler's armies. Negotiations cannot convince al Qaeda's leaders to lay down their arms. To say that force may sometimes be necessary is not a call to cynicism – it is a recognition of history; the imperfections of man and the limits of reason."[185]

The Cheneys' take on what makes the United States exceptional is based on a similar belief in the necessity of war. Their view is driven by the evil threats that exist outside U.S. borders: Hitler, the Soviet Union, Muslim terrorists, and Saddam Hussein's 1988 use of chemical weapons (with no mention of those weapons' origins in U.S. companies).[186] In fact, in contrast to Mugambi Jouet's book critiquing exceptionalism, in which foreign policy is almost an afterthought, for the Cheneys everything exceptional about the United States is war. Their book includes no mention of health, education, intellectual advancement, art, culture, technology, environmental protection, or quality of life -- only the idea of "freedom," which the authors, as is fairly typical, never define in any way. They only tell us that others do not have freedom, and that it is protected by wars -- the same wars that restrict rights to speak, to assemble, to report, to have a fair trial, to not be searched without a warrant, and to not be tortured or killed. These are all rights that the same book advocates violating.[187]

Lipset's book, in contrast, examines a range of subjects, the "double-edged sword" of his subtitle serving to justify much of the negative reality that he documents. Income inequality, high crime rates, low electoral participation, and other negative traits, he tells us, are the byproducts of very admirable norms and behaviors. We need to see the broader picture. The high crime rate, for example, Lipset writes, is the result of guaranteeing accused individuals due-process rights which somehow prevents gun control.[188] How an easy supply of guns facilitates and exacerbates crimes is fairly clear. But how the noble guaranteeing of rights to those accused of crimes prevents gun control is never explained. One might explain the prevalence of guns as the result of respecting people's rights to have guns. But this becomes circular reasoning rather than a double-edged sword, and it only very partially explains the crime rate.

Lipset explains poor marks in education, in part, as the product of a more inclusive effort to educate everyone. Yet other nations are as inclusive in elementary school, where the U.S. does especially poorly.

Lipset's sword balances a high divorce rate with "expressive individualism," but, he writes that "interpreting the higher American teenage pregnancy rate . . . is more difficult." By "interpreting," Lipset seems to mean "justifying." He goes on to explain the teen pregnancy rate as individualism leading to sex, and religiosity leading to a lack of birth control. He explains it just as well as he explains other things, but finds it more difficult to justify.[189]

This use of language is common. In 2015, Jay Parini wrote on CNN's website: "World War II may have been an American triumph of will and courage, but the Korean War is confusing, and students should consider its odd dimensions. Vietnam and Iraq are also complicated." Here "confusing" and "complicated" seem to be used as antonyms for "triumph of will and courage."[190]

Despite U.S. poverty, Lipset assures us that "the American emphasis on competitive individualism seems to have paid off. Corporate America, faced with strong foreign competition, has responded by becoming leaner and meaner, more efficient."[191] How that balances out the people hurt by the leanness and meanness is not explained. What actually seems exceptional about it is the uniquely U.S. habit of identifying with the well-being of corporations rather than people, and the assumption that foreigners must be competition. We have seen above that, even on these terms, the United States is not actually a world leader.

Lipset acknowledges that the United States has more inequality of "results" than other countries, but he swears (without evidence) that the United States has more equality of opportunity for upward mobility. Logically, such claims could only be true if the wealthy were falling while the poor were rising, which would not necessarily add up to a good side of a double-edged sword. In reality, as we have seen above, no such thing is actually true about U.S. society.

Mugambi Jouet's approach differs from Lipset's in that he seems interested in explaining the origins of negative traits, not justifying them. For Jouet, anti-intellectualism grew out of egalitarianism, while religious fundamentalism grew out of the separation of church and state. These are at best partial explanations, but at least they're not offered as claims that negative traits are unavoidable byproducts of something superior.

WAR TO END ALL PEACE

In exceptionalist nationalism, as perhaps in all nationalism, "we" are to adopt a first-person plural identity alive for centuries, so that "we fought the British" and "we won the Cold War." This self-identification, especially when combined with the belief in exceptional superiority, inclines the believer toward focusing on noble things "we" did, and away from shameful things "we" did, even though personally he or she deserves neither credit for the former nor blame for the latter. "The nationalist," wrote George Orwell, "not only does not disapprove of atrocities committed by his own side, but he has a remarkable capacity for not even hearing about them."[192]

On page 1 of the Cheneys' book: "We have guaranteed freedom, security, and peace for a larger share of humanity than has any other nation in all of history."[193] Such claims are, as here, generally not footnoted or explained. In the context of what follows it, the claim seems based largely on an analysis of World War II as the promotion of freedom and peace, and on a history of World War II that leaves out the lion's share of the Allies' fighting in Europe that was done by the Soviet Union.

The claim that "we" are the leading bringers of peace

and freedom may, of course, also be based on U.S. wars and weapons production since World War II. Certainly, if whoever fights the most wars and produces the most weapons brings the most peace and freedom to the earth, then the United States takes the title. But outside the United States, this logic is far from universally accepted -- quite the contrary. Most countries polled in December 2013 by Gallup called the United States the greatest *threat* to peace in the world.[194] A survey by Pew in 2017 found similar results.[195]

Since World War II, during what some U.S. academics think of as a golden age of peace, the U.S. military has killed or helped kill some 20 million people, overthrown at least 36 governments, interfered in at least 84 foreign elections, attempted to assassinate over 50 foreign leaders, and dropped bombs on people in over 30 countries.[196] The U.S. military costs nearly as much as the rest of the world's militaries combined, while the U.S., NATO members, and their allies account for three-quarters of the world's military spending. U.S. weapons dealing is exceptional in the sense of leading all others, but quite inclusive in terms of its clients. The United States, as noted above, as of 2017 provided weapons and in most cases training to 73 percent of the world's dictatorships.[197] It is certainly possible to find good results from some of this, but a clear-eyed understanding requires weighing the good against the bad. Is the globe that fails to appreciate all of this global policing made up of a bunch of ingrates? Or is the policing model seriously flawed?

Avoiding national criticism, or self-reflection on "us," risks allowing generosity to serve as a cover for a double standard. What might Americans think if another nation were to do some of its own freedom-promoting around the world? Such would be the behavior of a "rogue nation." Here is a count of military bases in the world that exist outside their nations' borders:[198]

United States -- 800
Russia -- 9
France -- 8

United Kingdom -- 8

Japan -- 1

South Korea -- 1

The Netherlands -- 1

India -- 1

Australia -- 1

Chile -- 1

Turkey -- 1

Israel -- 1

In 2007, the president of Ecuador told the United States that it could keep its base in Ecuador as long as Ecuador could have one in Miami, Florida.[199] The idea was, of course, ridiculous and outrageous.

Of the United Nations' 18 major human rights treaties, the United States is party to 5, fewer than any other nation on earth, except Bhutan (4), and tied with Malaya, Myanmar, and South Sudan, a country torn by warfare since its creation in 2011.[200] Is the United States functioning as the world's law enforcer from a location outside the world's laws? Or is something else going on?

That the United States has done something should not weigh for or against that thing. Actions should stand or fall on their own merits. But the Cheneys tell us we must see a "moral difference between an Iranian nuclear weapon and an American one." Must we, really? Either risks further proliferation, accidental use, use by a crazed leader, mass death and destruction, environmental disaster, retaliatory escalation, and apocalypse. One of those two nations has nuclear weapons[201], has used nuclear weapons[202], has provided the other with plans for nuclear weapons[203], has a policy of first-use of nuclear weapons[204], has leadership that sanctions the possession of nuclear weapons[205], and has frequently threated to use nuclear weapons[206]. I don't think those facts would make a nuclear weapon in the hands of the other country the least bit moral.

If you're wondering, U.S. presidents who have made specific public or secret nuclear threats to other nations, that we know of, have included Harry Truman, Dwight Eisenhower, Richard Nixon, George H.W. Bush, Bill Clinton, and Donald

Trump, while others, including Barack Obama, have frequently said things like "All options are on the table" in relation to Iran or another country.[207]

U.S. exceptionalism often does not take the form of viewing the United States as superior so much as viewing the United States as the only place that exists at all. In 2015, several state legislatures made efforts to keep Advanced Placement American History exams out of their high schools, because, in the words of Jane Robbins, a senior fellow at the American Principles Project, "every trace of American exceptionalism has been scrubbed."[208] The details this concern was raised over were all criticisms of the United States or lack of praise of the United States. There was no concern that the United States be described as superior to anywhere else or that anywhere else be mentioned at all. Rather, the pro-exceptionalism legislators and lobbyists suggested that because of U.S. exceptionalism, other countries need not be learned about.

Often when I suggest that war may be an institution

we actually want to outgrow and leave behind us, someone will say "What about the Revolution and the Civil War?" I've written at length in previous books about each popular war, including the most popular by far, World War II.[209] Below I'll debunk a few particular myths. I just want to note here how these arguments tend to erase the rest of the earth. Praise for the U.S. war for independence from Britain should have to begin, I think, with an explanation of how the Canadians or the Australians or the Indians are worse off for not having had one, as well as how accomplishing the same ends nonviolently would have been worse, and how such lessons relate to our much different current world.[210] Wonderful as well as horrible things followed the U.S. Revolution, but the first step in weighing its merits against theoretical or counterfactual alternatives should be comparing the U.S. experience with other countries'.

Similarly, slavery and serfdom once oppressed the majority of people on earth, and within a century those brutal institutions had been largely outlawed and in great measure ended. This was a global movement. In most places it did not involve civil wars. Yet, U.S. text books teach the history of one little corner of the world, with war after war after war as inevitable and unquestionable as the weather.

A list of all the nations where children regularly pledge allegiance to a flag would be pretty short, and not include any wealthy Western countries apart from the United States. While some countries have oaths to nations (Singapore) or dictators (North Korea), I can only find one country other than the United States where anyone claims that children regularly pledge allegiance to a flag: Mexico.[211] And I'm aware of two other countries that have a pledge of allegiance to a flag, although neither seems to use it as regularly as does the United States. Both are nations under heavy U.S. influence, and in both cases the pledge is relatively new. The Philippines has had a pledge of allegiance since 1996[212], and South Korea since 1972, but its current pledge since 2007.[213]

IS WHO WE ARE WHO WE ARE?

"That's not who we are," Barack Obama and other politicians have remarked after recounting widespread and long-lasting but unpleasant behaviors.[214]

Part of what came after the American Revolution was a new government that in some measure embodied the words that surrounded it, words that have come to be thought of as American ideals: freedom of religion and speech, equality, democracy, accountability, transparency, checks and balances. This was neither all hypocritical rhetoric nor all actual meritorious substance. The reality was and has been somewhere in between.

Yet almost from Day 1 exceptionalists who have recognized shortcomings have pined for the good old days which lacked any. A television series called *The Newsroom* premiered on the cable channel HBO on June 24, 2012, and the first episode opened with a panelist on stage being asked why the United States is the greatest country on earth. "It isn't," he replies to a stunned and scandalized audience, rattling off the U.S. failures to rank first in literacy, math, science, life expectancy, infant mortality, and median household income, while reaching top status in number of people incarcerated, military spending, and percentage of the public believing angels are real.

Then this straight-talking truth-bringer wistfully remarks: "It sure used to be." Without providing any details, he claims that the United States used to be the greatest country on earth and used to act for moral reasons and does so no longer. But when exactly was that age of moral greatness? Was it just a decade or so back, when the chief writer of *The Newsroom* Aaron Sorkin was depicting a very fictional and moral White House in another series called *The West Wing*? The U.S. wasn't tops in education or health then either. The point, I think, was not to communicate any such specific claim, but rather to abide by the requirement of exceptionalism that one balance any fault-finding with a claim of past and potentially future perfection.

Such perfection has always been worth aspiring to but, in reality, always quite a long ways off. On July 5, 1852, the formerly enslaved Frederick Douglass lavished praise on the founders of the United States before asking a troubling question:[215]

> What, to the American slave, is your 4th of July? I answer: a day that reveals to him, more than all other days in the year, the gross injustice and cruelty to which he is the constant victim. To him, your celebration is a sham; your boasted liberty, an unholy license; your national greatness, swelling vanity; your sounds of rejoicing are empty and heartless; your denunciations of tyrants, brass fronted impudence; your shouts of liberty and equality, hollow mockery; your prayers and hymns, your sermons and thanksgivings, with all your religious parade, and solemnity, are, to him, mere bombast, fraud, deception, impiety, and hypocrisy — a thin veil to cover up crimes which would disgrace a nation of savages. There is not a nation on the earth guilty of practices, more shocking and bloody,

than are the people of these United States, at this very hour.

Douglass believed the United States had created something wonderful but had left some people out of it. He also believed the United States to have excelled all others in the horror of its terrible crimes. Which is the "true" America, the bits it does well or those it does badly? The standard convention has been to follow Langston Hughes' generosity:

America never was America to me,
And yet I swear this oath—
America will be![216]

Such is the meaning given to Vietnam's Declaration of Independence of 1945 quoting from America's despite the United States' past and future displays of enormous contempt for the notion that all Vietnamese and Americans are "created equal."[217] According to General William Westmoreland, commander of U.S. forces in Vietnam from 1964 to 1968, "the Oriental doesn't put the same high price on life as does a Westerner. Life is plentiful. Life is cheap in the Orient."[218]

Such is also the meaning generally attributed to Lincoln's Gettysburg Address and to Martin Luther King, Jr's "I Have a Dream" speech. We often think of the United States as struggling to live up to its noble ideals. The reality is of course that the U.S. government and society have had noble and ignoble ideals and striven to meet and met both. Nobility and heroism have intermingled with cynicism, incompetence, and sadism. And some of it all has been extreme, exceptionally great or awful -- and much of it extremely well communicated, promoted, and advertised, for better and for worse.

ARE WE NOT WHAT WE ARE NOT?

Robert Jackson, Chief U.S. Prosecutor at the trials of Nazis for war and related crimes held in Nuremberg, Germany, following World War II, set a standard for the world: "If certain acts of violation of treaties are crimes, they are crimes whether the United States does them or whether Germany does them, and we are not prepared to lay down a rule of criminal conduct against others which we would not be willing to have invoked against us."

Among the trials held in Nuremberg was one of Nazi doctors accused of human experimentation and mass murder. This trial lasted from December 9, 1946, to August 20, 1947. An important witness provided by the American Medical Association was Dr. Andrew C. Ivy. He explained that Nazi doctors' actions "were crimes because they were performed on prisoners without their consent and in complete disregard for their human rights. They were not conducted so as to avoid unnecessary pain and suffering." In the April 27, 1947, *New York Times*, that newspaper's science editor Waldemar Kaempffert wrote that human experiments with syphilis would be valuable but "ethically impossible."

Dr. John C. Cutler read the short article. He was at the time engaged in giving syphilis to unsuspecting victims in Guatemala. He was doing this with the funding, knowledge, and support of his superiors at the U.S. Public Health Service. He called the *Times* article to the attention of Dr. John F. Mahoney, his director at the Venereal Diseases Research Laboratory of the Public Health Service. Cutler wrote to Mahoney that in light of the *Times* article, Cutler's work in Guatemala should be guarded with increased secrecy. Cutler had gone to Guatemala because he believed it was a place where he could get away with intentionally infecting people with syphilis in order to experiment with possible cures and placebos. He did not believe he could get away with such actions in the United States. In February 1947, Cutler had begun infecting female prostitutes with syphilis and using them to infect numerous men. In April he began infecting men directly. The motivation was to find better ways to cure syphilis in members of the U.S. military, which clearly was not considering ending its operations simply because the war had ended and the United Nations been established. Many U.S. doctors at this time considered the Nuremberg Code that came out of the Nazi trials to be "a good code for barbarians."

Many continued experimenting on humans for decades.

The United States had led the way in outlawing war in 1928 and in prosecuting war and related crimes in the 1940s. It even helped lead the way in developing ethical standards for doctors. But only very slowly are such standards applied to the United States itself. The International Criminal Court would not exist without past U.S. leadership, but there is little prospect of the United States joining or supporting it.

The United States is one of five nations with veto power in the U.N. Security Council. Since 1972, the U.S. has been far and away the leading user of that power. It has vetoed U.N. condemnation of South African apartheid, Israel's wars and occupations, chemical and biological weapons, nuclear weapons proliferation and first use and use against non-nuclear nations, U.S. wars in Nicaragua and Grenada and Panama, the U.S. embargo on Cuba, Rwandan genocide, the deployment of weapons in outerspace, etc.[219] And this is just scraping the surface. The five permanent members primarily use the veto power as an unrecorded threat of a veto made behind closed doors, and they use their power to keep many undesired topics off the public agenda entirely.[220]

The origin myths of U.S. exceptionalism are heavily focused on World War II, a war that is imagined in some ways as never having ended. The United States is still the victor. The losers are still the losers. The U.S. troops are still in Germany and Japan. The military machinery and the taxes to pay for it have never gone away. World War II is among the top, if not the very top, subjects of U.S. films and books. Hitler is the top reference in the demonizing of new enemies. And the idea that war is an acceptable answer to foreign conflicts is often unquestioned. But is it really an acceptable answer? Was it ever?

In Évian-les-Baines, France, in July 1938, the first international effort was made (or feigned) to alleviate a refugee crisis. The crisis was the Nazi treatment of Jews. The representatives of 32 nations and 63 organizations (plus some 200 journalists covering the event) were well aware of the Nazis' desire to expel all Jews from Germany and Austria, and somewhat aware that the fate that awaited them if not expelled was death. The decision of the conference was essentially to leave the Jews to their fate. (Only Costa Rica and the Dominican Republic increased their immigration quotas.) The decision to abandon the Jews was driven primarily by anti-Semitism, which was widespread among the diplomats in attendance and among the publics they represented.

These nations were represented at the Évian Conference: Australia, the Argentine Republic, Belgium, Bolivia, Brazil, United Kingdom, Canada, Chile, Colombia, Costa Rica, Cuba, Denmark, Dominican Republic, Ecuador, France, Guatemala, Haiti, Honduras, Ireland, Mexico, the Netherlands, New Zealand, Nicaragua, Norway, Panama, Paraguay, Peru, Sweden, Switzerland, the United States, Uruguay, and Venezuela. Italy refused to attend.

Australian delegate T. W. White said, without asking the native people of Australia: "as we have no real racial problem, we are not desirous of importing one."[221]

The dictator of the Dominican Republic viewed Jews as racially desirable, as bringing whiteness to a land with many people of African descent. Land was set aside for 100,000 Jews, but fewer than 1,000 ever arrived.[222]

In *The Jewish Trail of Tears The Evian Conference of July 1938*, Dennis Ross Laffer concludes that the conference was set up to fail and put on for show. Certainly it was proposed by and chaired by a representative of U.S. President Franklin Roosevelt who chose not to make the necessary efforts to aid Jewish refugees, before, during, or after the conference.[223]

"Popular support was reflected in various newspapers," writes Laffer. "Foreign correspondent, columnist and Pulitzer Prize winner Anne O'Hare

McCormick described the 'heartbreaking' scenes of long lines of Jews seeking visas from U.S. Consulates abroad while 'waiting in suspense' for the outcome of the Evian Conference. She believed that the issue facing America and the world was not how many 'unemployed' could be added to the national rolls of the unemployed. Rather, the world faced a fundamental 'test of civilization.' Could America accept the moral guilt, McCormick asked, if Germany was allowed to continue with its blatant 'policy of extermination' of the Jewish people?"[224]

America chose the moral guilt, although it avoids awareness of it (a moral guilt that I wish it were unnecessary to say does not somehow magically absolve the Nazis of their moral guilt). America rejected the Wagner-Rogers bill to admit more Jewish and non-Aryan refugees, but passed the Hennings Bill to allow unlimited numbers of British Christian children into the United States. A June 1938 Gallup poll found that seventy-two percent of Americans believed "we should not allow a larger number of Jewish exiles from Germany into the U.S."[225]

Hitler responded to news of the Evian Conference: "I can only hope and expect that the other world, which has such deep sympathy for these criminals [Jews], will at least be generous enough to convert this sympathy into practical aid. We, on our part, are ready to put all these criminals at the disposal of these countries, for all I care, even on luxury ships."[226]

"At stake at Evian were both human lives – and the decency and self-respect of the civilized world," writes Walter Mondale. "If each nation at Evian had agreed on that day to take in 17,000 Jews at once, every Jew in the Reich could have been saved."[227] Of course, with German expansion in the years ahead, the number of Jews and non-Jews subject to murder by the Nazis would grow to much more than 17,000 times 32.

Ervin Birnbaum was a leader on the *Exodus 1947*, a ship that carried Holocaust survivors to Palestine, and a Professor of Government in New York, Haifa, and Moscow Universities and Director of Projects at Ben Gurion's College of the Negev. He writes that, "the fact that the Evian Conference did not pass a resolution condemning the German treatment of Jews was widely used in Nazi propaganda and further emboldened Hitler in his assault on European Jewry leaving them ultimately subject to Hitler's 'Final Solution to the Jewish Question.'"[228] The U.S. Congress also failed to pass such a resolution.

Kristallnacht came in November 1938. And "in his Reichstag speech of January 30, 1939, Hitler used the world's reluctance to absorb Jewish refugees to legitimize the Nazi program of expulsion:

> It is a shameful spectacle to see how the whole democratic world is oozing sympathy for the poor tormented Jewish people, but remains hard-hearted and obdurate when it comes to aiding them — which is surely, in view of its attitude, an obvious duty. The arguments that are brought up as excuses for not helping them actually speak for us Germans and Italians. For this is what they say:

1. "We," that is the democracies, "are not in a position to take in the Jews." Yet in these empires there are not even ten people to the square kilometer. While Germany, with her 135 inhabitants to the square kilometer, is supposed to have room for them!

2. They assure us: We cannot take them unless Germany is prepared to allow them a certain amount of capital to bring with them as immigrants."[229]

The idea that the problem at Évian was ignorance of the Nazi agenda — were any scholar to make such an argument — would be undone by the minutes of the Bermuda Conference of 1943, held when government officials certainly knew about the genocide underway. The outcome of that conference, held by the U.S. and U.K., was the same as the one at Évian.

Jessie Wallace Hughan, founder of the War Resisters League, was very concerned in 1942 by stories of Nazi plans, no longer focused on expelling Jews but turning toward plans to murder them. Hughan believed that such a development appeared "natural, from their pathological point of view," and that it might really be acted upon if World War II continued. "It seems that the only way to save thousands and perhaps millions of European Jews from destruction," she wrote, "would be for our government to broadcast the promise" of an "armistice on condition that the European minorities are not molested any further. . . . It would be very terrible if six months from now we should find that this threat has literally come to pass without our making even a gesture to prevent it." When her predictions were fulfilled only too well by 1943, she wrote to the U.S. State Department and the New York Times: "two million [Jews] have already died" and "two million more will be killed by the end of the war." She warned that military successes against Germany would just result in further scapegoating of Jews. "Victory will not save them, for dead men cannot be liberated," she wrote.

Nicholson Baker provides additional perspective:

Anthony Eden, Britain's foreign secretary, who'd been tasked by [Prime Minister Winston] Churchill with handling queries about refugees, dealt coldly with one of many important delegations, saying that any diplomatic effort to obtain the release of the Jews from Hitler was "fantastically impossible." On a trip to the United States, Eden candidly told Cordell Hull, the secretary of state, that the real difficulty with asking Hitler for the Jews was that "Hitler might well take us up on any such offer, and there simply are not enough ships and means of transportation in the world to handle them." Churchill agreed. "Even were we to obtain permission to withdraw all the Jews," he wrote in reply to one pleading letter, "transport alone presents a problem which will be difficult of solution." Not enough shipping and transport? Two years earlier, the British had evacuated nearly 340,000 men from the beaches of Dunkirk in just nine days. The U.S. Air Force had many thousands of new planes. During even a brief armistice, the Allies could have airlifted and transported refugees in very large numbers out of the German sphere.[230]

Dick and Liz Cheney feature the tragedy of Anne Frank in their World War II U.S. origins tale. Yet, a ship of Jewish refugees from Germany was chased away from Miami by the Coast Guard.[231] The U.S. and other nations refused to accept most Jewish refugees, and the majority of the U.S. public supported that position.[232] The U.S. engaged in no diplomatic or military effort to save the victims in the Nazi concentration camps. Anne Frank's family was denied U.S. visas.[233] And several times the number of people killed in the camps were killed outside the camps in the war.[234]

INNOCENTS ABROAD

In war (and if the state of war is permanent then so is this) all of "our" flaws must be hidden and all of "their" flaws trumpeted from a mountaintop. Above all, "we" must only act defensively, never aggressively. When President Trump made a trip to Asia in 2017, threatening North Korea with war, he stopped first at Pearl Harbor to cloak himself in the mantle of defensiveness and innocence. That the Japanese committed an evil and murderous act of aggression at Pearl Harbor in 1941 might seem to have little bearing on 2017. Yet it is important, in fact centrally vital, to U.S. exceptionalism, that the crime of the Japanese be remembered, and that as little attention as possible be paid to the facts that the United States had trained Japan in militarism and expansion[235]; that the United States had knowingly threatened, antagonized, and provoked Japan[236]; that President Roosevelt had told Prime Minister Churchill that "everything was to be done to force an incident[237];"that the United States had provided planes and trainers and pilots to China; that the United States had blockaded Japan[238]; that Roosevelt's prediction to his cabinet of a Japanese attack was off by only six days[239]; and that the top headline on the *Honolulu Advertiser* on November 30, 1941, read, "Japanese May Strike Over Weekend." [240]

Actual history is never as clean and simple as the cartoon versions. But the Cheneys' worldview requires that it be. Weakness is always wrong. Strength is always right. Cheney blames President Kennedy for not bombing Cuba in support of the Bay of Pigs invasion.[241] That we now know that there were already at the time nuclear weapons in Cuba, that the major attack the CIA was hoping to force Kennedy into would have risked nuclear apocalypse, is no matter. Kennedy showed weakness, and one must only show strength. One must demand respect and wreak vicious vengeance on any who disrespect you, even if everybody dies. It's the creed of the duelist, the drug lord, the mafioso, and perhaps the exceptionalist.

It is not actually a defensive position. Cheney cites approvingly a Regional Defense Strategy published by the Pentagon he ran in January 1993, which listed four "defense" goals, only one of which was defensive. The other three goals were to strengthen alliances, preclude any hostile power from dominating any region critical to "our interests," and "reducing sources of regional instability."[242] Some of those sound like admirable goals for diplomats. They're not goals so easily achieved with bombs and guns.

While Cheney admits that all the 2002-2003 tales of vast stockpiles of "weapons of mass destruction" in Iraq were false, he still claims that "Saddam's Iraq was the most likely place for terrorists to gain access to and knowledge of such weapons."[243] While that was the furthest thing from the truth in 2002, and while it is simply not possible to gain access to weapons that do not exist, it did become true as a result of the war that Iraq was in later years, and still is, a top generator of non-state political violence, a.k.a. terrorism.[244]

Terrorism has predictably increased during the war on terrorism (as measured by the Global Terrorism Index). 99.5 percent of terrorist attacks occur in countries engaged in wars and/or engaged in abuses such as imprisonment without trial, torture, or lawless killing. The highest rates of terrorism are in "liberated" and "democratized" Iraq and

Afghanistan. The terrorist groups responsible for the most terrorism around the world have grown out of U.S. wars against terrorism. Those wars themselves have left numerous just-retired top U.S. government officials and even a few U.S. government reports describing military violence as counterproductive, as creating more enemies than are killed.[245]

Attacking terrorists tends to produce more terrorists who must be attacked. It's regretfully a vicious cycle, but of course there's nothing else that can possibly be done. Or is there? If "we" ever tried to learn from other countries, one of those countries might be Spain. On March 11, 2004, Al Qaeda bombs killed 191 people in Madrid, Spain, just before an election in which one party was campaigning against Spain's participation in the U.S.-led war on Iraq. The people of Spain voted the Socialists into power, and they removed all Spanish troops from Iraq by May. There were no more bombs. This history stands in strong contrast to that of Britain, the United States, and other nations that have responded to blowback with more war, often producing more blowback.

The Western arrogance of feeling that it has everything to teach others and nothing to learn from them is not just. A true revolution of values will lay hand on the world order and say of war, "This way of settling differences is not just." --Martin Luther King Jr.[246]

It is generally considered inappropriate to pay attention to the Spanish example, and U.S. media has even tried reporting on this history in Spain as if the opposite of what happened happened. In 2016, National Public Radio (NPR) suggested that ISIS might attack the United States in order to elect Donald Trump who might boost ISIS recruiting by being more aggressive toward Muslims. NPR offered the example of Spain, claiming that terrorism had resulted in the more pro-war candidate winning, the opposite of what actually happened.[247]

SORRY SEEMS TO BE THE HARDEST WORD

While the exceptionalist state must always act defensively, its defensive tools must be force and intimidation, never giving an inch, and -- most of all -- never, ever apologizing. While this belief has been expressed by many, one of its clearest statements came from then-Vice President George H.W. Bush while he campaigned successfully for president in 1988. The U.S. Navy had shot down an Iranian passenger plane, killing 290 people, including 66 children. "I will never apologize for the United States," Bush said, "Ever. I don't care what the facts are."[248]

While Barack Obama was president, making speeches with vaguely conciliatory statements and acknowledgement of past actions, including the CIA's 1953 overthrow of Iran's democracy, it became common in U.S. media to denounce Obama's "Apology Tour." However, Obama never actually apologized for any past actions by the U.S. government, not even when he visited Hiroshima.[249] He did apologize for one of a great many of his own drone strikes that killed a great many civilians. It was a strike that had killed an Italian and an American.[250]

President Obama had made clear to the *New York*

Times just before his second election in 2012 that he regularly looked through a list of men, women, and children on Tuesdays, picking which ones to have killed with missiles from drones.[251] He reportedly — and he did not dispute the report — remarked during that reelection campaign that he was "really good at killing people."[252] Two weeks after killing a man named Anwar al-Awlaki as punishment for things he had written and said, Obama's subordinates killed Awlaki's 16-year-old American son Abdulrahman al-Awlaki. Obama campaign senior adviser and former White House Press Secretary Robert Gibbs, when asked about this killing, replied with the opposite of an apology. He said that Abdulrahman "should have [had] a far more responsible father." Donald Trump was president when a U.S. raid killed Abdulrahman's little sister.[253]

Those sorts of incidents, while troubling, are readily forgiven or rationalized as unfortunate side-effects or "collateral damage." What is not forgiven is questioning U.S. exceptionalism. "I believe in American exceptionalism with every fiber of my being," President Obama reassured us. And at a 2012 Republican presidential primary debate, at least part of the audience cheered for both peace and war proposals. But when one of the candidates proposed applying "the golden rule" to other countries -- to treat them as one's own country would like to be treated -- the crowd booed.[254] A hall full of Republicans in South Carolina booed a moral lesson attributed to Jesus Christ, apparently in support of the highest commandment of all: Thou shalt not place the United States on the same level with any other country.

ENGAGED BUT UNILATERAL

Hilde Eliassen Restad's 2015 book *American Exceptionalism: An Idea That Made a Nation and Remade the World*, argues that U.S. foreign policy has always and consistently been an embodiment of exceptionalism, internationally engaged but "unilateral."[255] Another term might be "imperial." Restad rejects the notion that the U.S. has gone through cycles of being more an exemplary "city on a hill" and isolationist on the one hand, versus missionary and internationalist on the other. Instead, Restad traces a consistent imperial approach to the world -- a world in which Native Americans and Mexicans exist and count as part of the world, so that U.S. imperialism didn't begin only after the creation of its North American empire. The approach of "unilateral internationalism" stems from a time of British settler colonial exceptionalism right up through the current U.S. exceptionalism that we falsely imagine to alter significantly with the partisanship of each president.

The myth of U.S. "isolationism" feeds a view that empire was somehow thrust upon a reluctant monkish hermit rather than being vigorously pursued from day one. It also supports the myth that the U.S. war for independence was just a U.S. rebellion, rather than part of a war between England and France. And then there's the origin myth which holds that World War II transformed U.S. foreign policy. On the contrary, Restad documents a constant U.S. approach to the world, rejecting the

League of Nations because it would have put the United States on the same level with other nations, but accepting the United Nations (and the IMF and the World Bank and NATO) because it did no such thing. The U.N. was created with U.S. veto power and the ability of the U.S. to opt out of the International Court of Justice and any U.N. treaty or action. It was based on U.S. soil and subject to U.S. financing. Under these conditions, Restad argues, the League of Nations would have passed through the U.S. Senate in 1919.[256]

U.S. foreign policy during the Cold War was driven by U.S. exceptionalist imperialism, not by fear of or opposition to the Soviet Union, as was revealed to some by U.S. foreign policy's virtually unaltered continuation despite the ending of the Soviet Union. The expected major military reductions and "peace dividends" never materialized. Similarly, U.S. foreign policy during the War on Terrorism has not been a counterproductive effort to reduce terrorism, but rather a continuation of exceptionalism in new packaging -- and of the war-profiteering thereby justified.

The U.S. position as "superpower" is supposed to have been achieved reluctantly and altruistically. "We did not seek the position," wrote Dick and Liz Cheney following centuries of steady pursuit of expansion and dominance by the U.S. government.[257] The Cheneys avoid the reality of U.S. history. For example, more Filipinos died in the first day of fighting off their U.S. benefactors in 1899 than Americans would die storming the beaches at Normandy.[258] Many more Filipinos died in the U.S. war to liberate them than had been killed in three-and-a-half centuries of the Spanish rule from which they were liberated.[259]

Senator Albert Beveridge of Indiana toured the Philippines in 1899 and reported to the Senate that "this is the divine mission of America," without which "the world would relapse into barbarism and night."[260] In the days and years that followed, many Filipinos were discovered to be in need of waterboarding. U.S. troops sang a song about providing the water torture to the Filipinos. Here's a verse:

Oh pump it in him till he swells like a toy balloon.
The fool pretends that liberty is not a precious boon.
But we'll contrive to make him see the beauty of it
soon.
Shouting the battle cry of freedom.[261]

Freedom. Does the word have meaning? What should that meaning be? Patrick Henry (or the embellished mythical character we know as Patrick Henry), in a speech composed decades after his death, spoke of "liberty" from Britain, even while the real Patrick Henry owned people as slaves.[262] Franklin Roosevelt spoke of freedom of speech and religion, and freedom from want and fear.[263] Where do the United States and the world stand now on those four freedoms?

The Puritans were extremist opponents of enlightenment out to Make Christianity Great Again. The view that they shared with most of the early settler colonists (though clearly much moderated in the Quakers) was one of divine right to imperial expansion and ethnic cleansing.

The U.S. nation was born in war and claimed as the spoils of that war a new freedom to expand westward. The U.S. Civil War arose not out of a conflict over slavery in existing states, but out of a conflict over the question of slavery in newly conquered lands -- combined with the absolutely unquestionable and universal agreement on the need to conquer new lands.

Out of the Constitution and Bill of Rights came the wonderful benefits of the (always partial) recognition of freedoms of speech, assembly, religion, etc. But out of these, and an infinitely complex collection of other factors, came also some perverse results. Freedom of religion became the freedom to invent and buy into new religions, which amounts to the acceptance of claiming things without evidence, choosing to believe those things, and treating that choice as your sacred right. Believers that Saddam Hussein had nukes in 2003 and Barack Obama was born in Nigeria and climate change is not real and Vladimir Putin stole the 2016 U.S. election exercise this same right.

So do believers in U.S. exceptionalism. If you give someone their first donut and they declare it the greatest donut in the world, you can probably make them see the weakness of their claim. But if someone who's never lived outside the United States (or its military bases) claims that the United States is the greatest country on earth, good luck trying to change their mind. They're probably not making an empirical statement at all. They're exercising their inalienable right to believe what they feel like believing. And since their opinion doesn't harm you, what right have you got to object to it?

Or does it harm you after all? We'll consider that in Part III below.

III. *The Damage Exceptionalism Does*

So what's the big stinking deal? Some people think their country is super great and the facts say otherwise, and their knowledge of history is a little selective -- who cares? Fans of lousy sports teams will declare their team the best, and nobody makes a big brouhaha over it. People will declare their town or their children or their car the greatest on earth, and felony charges are not brought against them as a result. What's the difference here? And shouldn't people be left happy in their delusions? If everyone on earth believed their own corner of the earth to be the very "greatest," what a wonderful world it would be, right?

Some have seriously tried to make this case, or one similar to it, and I've found it completely unconvincing.[264] If everyone on earth thought like exceptionalists, the earth would be a raging conflict of competing empires. Citizens or elites of past empires may have thought as exceptionalists.

We have had passed down to us exceptionalist statements from the British and the Romans, for cxample. But few will argue that empires of the past, much less empires today, much less a world of rival empires, do no harm.

LIVES THAT DON'T MATTER

What we're dealing with is not just valuing the United States, but also devaluing the rest of the world -- and not just as observers, but as people who believe they have the right, if not the duty, to impose their will on the rest of the world. Exceptionalism is an attitude that tends to include arrogance, ignorance, and aggression, and these tend to do a great deal of damage.

In recent polling on possible future wars, a majority in the United States is willing to support an air attack, even a nuclear attack, on a foreign country, such as Iran or North Korea, that kills 100,000 civilians if it is an alternative to a ground attack that could kill 20,000 Americans.[265] In fact, the U.S. public has largely sat by for the past 17 years of wars in which the nations attacked have suffered tens and hundreds of times more deaths than the U.S. military.[266] Americans overwhelmingly tell pollsters that it is fine to kill non-Americans with U.S. drones, but illegal to kill U.S. citizens.[267] Keith Payne, a drafter of the 2018 U.S. Nuclear Posture Review, back in 1980, parroting *Dr. Strangelove*, defined success to allow up to 20 million dead Americans as the price for killing a much higher number of non-Americans.[268] The U.S. government has placed compensation for an Iraqi life at no more than $15,000, but the value of a U.S. life at no less than $5 million.[269]

When people ask how President Harry Truman could have used nuclear weapons that killed so many Japanese people unless he actually believed he was saving at least some significant number of U.S. lives, they are assuming that Truman placed some positive value on the life of a Japanese person. Truman was the same man who had earlier remarked, "If we see that Germany is winning we ought to help Russia and if Russia is winning we ought to help Germany, and that way let them kill as many as possible."[270] U.S. Secretary of State Madeleine Albright famously remarked that the deaths of a half million Iraqi children was "worth it," without really being pressed to explain what the "it" was.[271] During the war on Vietnam, the U.S. military bragged on a weekly basis about how many people it killed. In recent wars, it has avoided mentioning that topic. But in neither case does it weigh the non-U.S. lives taken against whatever the supposed good is that's being attempted, as it might do if it believed those lives had any value.

This is where exceptionalism looks like a form of bigotry. One type of person is much more valuable. The other 96 percent of humanity is just not worth very much. If people in the United States valued all human lives equally, or even remotely close to equally, discussions of foreign aid funded by the U.S. government would sound very different. The U.S. government budget devotes less than 1 percent to foreign aid (including weapons "aid") but the U.S. public on average believes that 31 percent of the budget goes to foreign aid.[272] Reducing this mythical generosity is extremely popular with the U.S. public.[273] The U.S. public usually sees itself as enormously generous to the rest of the world, but often believes its imagined generosity to be unappreciated. Several years into the war on Iraq that began in 2003, a plurality in the United States believed, not only that Iraqis should be grateful, but that Iraqis were in fact grateful for a war that had scholars using the term "sociocide" to describe its impact on Iraqi society.[274]

U.S. exceptionalism does not just devalue the individual lives of others. It also devalues the earth as a whole. U.S. policy is generally not shaped by concern for its impact on the planet's environment. And the attitude of constant competition for the most growth on a finite planet is destructive and ultimately self-defeating. As an exceptionalist -- or, as the U.S. government would call the same attitude in someone else, a rogue -- the United States keeps itself out of more international treaties than do its peers. It also keeps itself out of the jurisdiction of courts of international law and arbitration. This position hurts the U.S. public, by denying it new developments in human rights. And it deals a severe blow to the rule of law elsewhere, because of the prominence and power of the world's leading rogue nation.

The U.S. Constitution and U.S. laws are not independently updated to match world standards. In fact, it seems that the further the United States' ancient constitution falls behind, the more it is treated as a sacred relic never to be improved. In an exceptionalist outlook, it is the responsibility of foreigners to learn from the U.S. Constitution, not the responsibility of the U.S. public to learn from the constitutions or laws more recently developed elsewhere. If you give rights to the environment or to indigenous people, you're being silly. If we give rights to corporations, we're being American -- and that's not to be questioned. End of discussion.

In an exceptionalist worldview it is of absolutely zero interest that many countries have figured out big advances in healthcare coverage or gun control or fast trains or green energy or drug treatment. Why would anyone in the United States care to hear such news! A study of presidents' state of the union speeches between 1934 and 2008 found 2,500 mentions of other countries, but only 3 suggestions that the United States might learn anything from any of them.[275] As the Greatest Nation on Earth it is the rightful U.S. role to continue bumbling along with its always greatest policies, even if those policies kill us -- but especially if they merely kill other people.

The United States not only turns away ideas. It also turns away actual emergency aid offered by other countries following natural disasters.[276] What are human lives in comparison with national pride?

EVIL OF TWO LESSERS

One enduring but disastrous U.S. policy is its duopolistic system of two political parties. While over 40 percent of the public identifies as independent of either big party, nobody outside of either big party is allowed in presidential primary debates or provided equal coverage by big media in Congressional elections.[277]

The two big parties disagree on some important issues, but fundamentally agree on exceptionalism and on some of the policies it drives, such as militarism. One party currently seems focused on building walls, deporting families, banning certain immigrants, threatening catastrophic wars, and viciously competing with other nations' economies. The other has spent the past year obsessed with creating a new cold war with Russia and developing a climate in which any sort of contact with Russians is viewed as potentially treasonous. These behaviors are generally in character for these two parties and perfectly in line with exceptionalism.

As a fan of the mechanism in the U.S. Constitution called impeachment, I've drafted numerous articles of impeachment for President Donald Trump. [278] Some of the well-known offenses have little to do with exceptionalism: financial corruption in violation of both the foreign and domestic emoluments clauses of the Constitution, for example. The overwhelming preference of activist groups and media outlets for consideration of the foreign emoluments clause over the domestic one has shades of exceptionalism, as does the preference of the leading Democrats for avoiding the whole topic (and each of the following topics) and focusing on Russia.

Other impeachable offenses committed by Donald Trump look clearly exceptionalist. These include his efforts to ban Muslims from entering the United States. Trump had openly campaigned for office promising a "total and complete shutdown of Muslims entering the United States." Once in office, he created an executive order that his advisor Rudy Giuliani, said on *Fox News* had been drafted after Trump had asked him for the best way to create a Muslim ban "legally."[279] The order targeted several majority-Muslim countries for restrictions on immigration to the United States, but made allowances for people of minority religions within those countries. Trump told the *Christian Broadcasting Network* that Christian refugees would be given priority.[280] When a federal court stopped this order from taking effect, President Trump issued a new one containing, in the words of his advisor Stephen Miller "minor technical differences."[281]

Another Trump offense is his incitement of violence combined with his encouragement of hatred toward immigrants and other groups. He famously claimed that Mexican immigrants consist of drug dealers, criminals, and rapists.[282] He also issued a pardon for former sheriff of Maricopa County, Arizona, Joe Arpaio, who had been convicted of contempt for failure to comply with a court order in a case charging him with racial discrimination. Arpaio was open about his commission of the underlying crime, for which he was found guilty in a civil suit. His contempt conviction was for continuing to engage in racial profiling, violating an order to cease doing so. Arpaio set up a prison that he called a concentration camp. It had a high death rate with deaths often unexplained. He enclosed Latino prisoners with electric fencing.[283]

The U.S. Supreme Court ruled in *Brandenberg v. Ohio* in 1969 that "advocacy directed to inciting or producing imminent lawless action . . . likely to incite or produce such action" is not protected by the First Amendment.[284] Yet, Trump, while campaigning for office, made numerous statements like this one: "If you see somebody getting ready to throw a tomato, knock the crap out of them. I promise you, I will pay for the legal fees."[285] Or this one: "You see, in the good old days, law enforcement acted a lot quicker than this. A lot quicker. In the good old days, they'd rip him out of that seat so fast — but today, everybody's politically correct."[286] Numerous incidents of violence followed these comments. John Franklin McGraw punched a man in the face at a Trump event, and then told *Inside Edition* that "The next time we see him, we might have to kill him." Trump said that he was considering paying McGraw's legal bills.[287]

Since Trump's election and inauguration, his comments appearing to incite violence have continued, as have incidents of violence in which those participating in violence have pointed to Trump as justification. In August 2017, participants in a fascist rally in Charlottesville, Va., credited President Trump with boosting their cause. Their violence included actions that have led to a murder charge. President Trump publicly minimized the offense and sought to blame "many sides."[288]

It's not just groups of people Trump threatens, but the species of homo sapiens along with other species of life on earth. On December 6, 2009, on page 8 of the *New York Times* a letter to then-President Barack Obama printed as an advertisement and signed by Donald Trump called climate change an immediate challenge. "Please don't postpone the earth," it read. "If we fail to act now, it is scientifically irrefutable that there will be catastrophic and irreversible consequences for humanity and our planet."[289] An overwhelming consensus of climate scientists agreed with and still agrees with that statement. And Obama indeed failed to act in any way comparable to the urgent need. But, as president, Trump has refused to take any significant steps to protect the earth's climate, and has taken many steps to endanger it, including by seeking to de-fund the Environmental Protection Agency and to censor its publications. Trump has issued an executive order curbing enforcement of climate regulations. He has withdrawn the United States from the Paris Climate Agreement. He has disbanded the Advisory Committee for the Sustained National Climate Assessment. He has canceled a study of the health impacts of mountain-top removal. The prosecutor for the International Criminal Court has written that environmental crimes are crimes against humanity[290], but of course that's not relevant for the Greatest Nation on Earth.

Then there's Trump's lack of interest in preparing for or responding to hurricanes, including Harvey and Maria -- the latter so devastating to Puerto Rico. The Federal Emergency Management Agency (FEMA) was without a new director until June 2017. The National Hurricane Center was without a head from May 2017 through the time of Hurricane Harvey in August 2017. On August 15, 2017, President

Trump issued an executive order that rejected the Federal Flood Risk Management Standard, which had been established by executive order in 2015, and which required that infrastructure be built to withstand flooding.[291] When Hurricane Harvey hit, FEMA proposed that private individuals fund and perform relief efforts, and fell far short of meeting needs itself.[292] With an opportunity to learn from mistakes and another month to prepare, Trump's performance displayed even more reckless disregard for human life when Hurricane Maria threatened and struck Puerto Rico in September 2017. Trump's even worse performance was widely attributed to his apparent ignorance of the fact that Puerto Ricans are U.S. citizens.[293]

Beyond these exceptionalist offenses are the quintessentially exceptionalist, traditional, bi-partisan outrages for which any recent president could have been impeached: illegal wars, illegal threats of wars, drone strikes, mass surveillance, etc.

Traditionally the House of Representatives impeaches officials for alleged damage to the people of the United States. But my concern here is also the damage done to people not of the United States or imagined to not really be of the United States, such as the people of Puerto Rico, potential Muslim immigrants, recent immigrants, people not appearing to fit the image of an American conceived by a fascist, people living in low coastal areas of the earth, Latinos living in Arizona, and people living under U.S. missiles and bombs.

The Democratic Party has managed, in the face of these outrages, to turn its "resistance" to Trump into an exceptionalist, xenophobic, hatemongering build-up to a risk of nuclear war. In January 2007, after voters said they'd given the Democratic Party majorities in order to end the war on Iraq, the Chair of the House Democratic Caucus Rahm Emanuel made clear that Democrats would keep the war going in order to "oppose" it in elections two years later. The *Washington Post*'s David Ignatius had dinner with Emanuel, and reported: "The secret for the Democrats, says Emanuel, is to remain the party of reform and change. The country is angry, and it will only get more so as the problems in Iraq deepen. Don't look to Emanuel's Democrats for solutions on Iraq. It's Bush's war, and as it splinters the structure of GOP power, the Democrats are waiting to pick up the pieces."[294] This seems to be the 2017-2018 Democratic plan with Donald Trump: Keep him around, and run in future elections as the people who may not be much but are not him.[295]

As documented in John Nichols' book *The Genius of Impeachment*,[296] the U.S. Congress has used impeachment a great many times, against presidents and many other officials, often creating effective pressure for reform prior to actually impeaching. It's a process that has sometimes taken months, other times years. But the U.S. government would be even less representative than it is of the public will without this history.

Moves to impeach presidents, including Truman and Nixon, did significant good. Popular, and not strictly partisan, movements advanced principled demands around substantive abuses of power. While the worst war crimes were not passed as articles of impeachment, they were, at least with Nixon, part of the discussion. The results included, not just the end of particular abuses, but the creation of a climate in which others expected to be held accountable.

The impeachment of Bill Clinton, in contrast, focused with such hypocrisy, partisanship, and vindictiveness on such a lesser charge -- with serious offenses, readily available, never entering the discussion -- that the result was not only no conviction in the Senate and no reform in the government, but also a horribly damaging aversion to the tool of impeachment.

The refusal of Congress to meet the public demand for the impeachment of George W. Bush[297] cemented in place a sense of presidential impunity that has been flaunted by Bush, Obama, and now Trump. This has helped to transfer powers from Congress to the White House, and Congress members' diminishing identification with their branch of government (together with the increase in "campaign contributions") has radically increased their identification with their political parties. This process erodes representative government.

Impeachment and removal of Trump on the grounds discussed above, if created by public demand, would create good precedents, including the threat of a similar impeachment hanging over the head of Mike Pence or whoever next enters the oval office. Allowing these abuses to go unchecked, in contrast, risks nuclear and environmental apocalypse and guarantees severe suffering for millions. It virtually guarantees that the office of the presidency will be a tyrannical institution, no matter the merits of the man or woman who enters into it.

What is nowhere to be found on a serious list of Trump's impeachable offenses is Russia. But the same party that in 2016 found one of the only candidates on earth who could have lost an election to Trump has focused on the one charge against Trump that can backfire in a failure to convict and/or a war with a nuclear-armed nation.

The focus of the Democratic Party is on what many call a Russian "Pearl Harbor"[298] or "act of war"[299] against the United States, feeding right into Trump's own new policies of declaring cyber- and other crimes to be "acts of war" to be responded to with actual *war*.[300] This type of impeachment campaign, or even non-impeachment criticism campaign or permanent election campaign, risks getting us all killed. It also risks a failure to convict due to lack of evidence -- which failure would truly entrench dictatorial powers beyond any likely reform.

"Russiagate" was begun as a distraction from the content of Democratic Party emails, which documented unfair treatment of candidate Bernie Sanders.[301] The claim that either the Russian government or Trump, much less both, had anything to do with leaking those emails has never been proven, and is very unlikely to be. But if it were proven, it would be one more outrage to pile onto a list that includes the mistreatment of Sanders that the emails confirmed. Other serious outrages:

- The massive boost that corporate media chose to give to Donald Trump.[302]
- The intimidation and incitement to violence engaged in by candidate Trump. (See above.)
- The racist removal of voters from the roles by Republican governors and legislatures.[303]
- The unverifiable vote counting, and the failure to do proper counts even where possible.[304]
- The denial of a popular outcome by the Electoral College.[305]
- The exclusion of most candidates from the media and the televised debates.[306]
- The gargantuan financial corruption.[307]
- The hurdles placed in the way of registering to vote.[308]
- The ID laws and other hurdles placed in the way of voting.[309]

This was not an election system that could be noticeably worsened or improved by a single act of whistleblowing, no matter how inappropriate the source.

Nor have we yet seen evidence that would hold up in a court or in the U.S. Senate to prove that the Russian government organized any serious campaign on social media that could possibly have had any effect on the election, much less that it did so together with Trump. The fact that Russian state media outlets openly tended to prefer Trump to Clinton had no major impact on the election, involved Trump in no impeachable offense, and parallels the sorts of positions that U.S. state and private media outlets routinely take in elections around the world.[310]

That the United States government has in recent decades taken more serious steps to interfere in 84 elections including in Russia, and actually overthrown 36 governments, attempted to assassinate over 50 foreign leaders, and bombed over 30 countries,[311] does not in any way excuse similar crimes by others. But, given this reality, Russia provides a model of restraint that could be followed. For all the corrupt, anti-democratic, and militarist failings of the Russian government, without that government's restraint -- as the United States launches war after war, moves missiles to Russia's borders[312], bombs Russian fighters in Syria[313], instigates a coup in Ukraine[314], and accuses Russia of an action that the United States commits routinely -- we would not be here reading these words.

I'm using recent examples to describe a long-standing pattern. The two big political parties claim to be bitter enemies, diametrically opposed in their agendas, gridlocked with an absolute absence of overlap or agreement.[315] And yet they harmoniously roll through the Congress more and more military spending[316], surveillance powers[317], and so forth. And their opposing initiatives share something fundamental in common: U.S. exceptionalism. Whether you believe the danger to the unsullied U.S. "democracy" comes from Muslim terrorists or the monster of the North known as Vladimir Putin, you can agree that foreign demons must be kept out -- out of our airports, our elections, our televisions, and our towns.

In fact, the Pentagon and the weapons profiteers

would like you to be concerned about *both* dangers, Muslims *and* Russians. In May 2017 the *Politico* newspaper reported on Pentagon testimony in Congress to the effect that Russia had a superior and threatening military, but followed that with this: "'This is the "Chicken-Little, sky-is-falling" set in the Army,' the senior Pentagon officer said. 'These guys want us to believe the Russians are 10 feet tall. There's a simpler explanation: The Army is looking for a purpose, and a bigger chunk of the budget. And the best way to get that is to paint the Russians as being able to land in our rear and on both of our flanks at the same time. What a crock.'"

Politico then cited a less-than-credible "study" of Russian military superiority and aggression and added: "While the reporting about the Army study made headlines in the major media, a large number in the military's influential retired community, including former senior Army officers, rolled their eyes."[318]

MILITARY INDUSTRIAL EXCEPTIONALISM

As mentioned above, the U.S. public stands out in its support for militarism, its belief that wars are needed, its acceptance of "preemptively" attacking nations, and its disdain for requiring UN authorization of such attacks.[319] Another survey that confirms the same bias is the Gallup poll in 2014 that found over twice the percentage in the United States as in many other nations declaring that they "would fight in a war for their country."[320] What prevents most such willing war participants from finding the nearest recruiting station is not explained, but their desire to imagine themselves as war makers fits with their society's acceptance of wars, as well as with the advertising schemes of groups like the National Rifle Association (NRA), which produces videos with celebrities demanding more wars, as a means of selling more guns domestically.[321]

The acceptance of wars is absolutely dependent on the identification with a national government. Just as sports fan will declare "We scored!" while seated in front of a television, a war fan will announce "We bombed them!" and identify with one "team." But only in the United States do public "democratic" debates include discussions of whether to launch more wars, as mainstream U.S. foreign policy journals today discuss whether to attack Iran or North Korea.[322] Nowhere else on earth can you find a presidential election debate containing a question like this one asked by a CNN debate moderator in 2015:[323]

> People admire and respect and are inspired by your life story, your kindness, your evangelical core support. We're talking about ruthless things tonight—carpet bombing, toughness, war. And people wonder, could you do that? Could you order air strikes that would kill innocent children by not the scores, but the hundreds and the thousands? Could you wage war as a commander-in-chief?

If you're not mean enough to thoughtlessly slaughter

thousands of children, what kind of exceptionalist are you? Not a presidential one! At least not according to CNN. Also according to the U.S. media, the U.S. has not only a right to kill people anywhere, as "needed," but can suffer as the victim of "aggression" and respond with "defense" anywhere, so that Syrian attacks on U.S. troops *in Syria* have been generally referred to as Syrian aggression[324], as have interactions between U.S. and Russian planes near the border of Russia been referred to as Russian aggression.[325]

There are a couple of senses in which the planet could not survive two or more nations behaving like the United States. One is in terms of the environmental impact of war-making. The other is in terms of the wars produced and the risk of one or more wars becoming nuclear. In the United States the massing of thousands of troops and major weaponry on other nations' borders halfway around the globe is understood as "defensive,"[326] but if anyone else were to try such a thing it would be thought of as offensive. In morality it is common to suppose that

a good behavior is one that would do more good
if emulated by others. The only way to square this
with U.S. behavior is to declare the United States
exceptional and its lawlessness as being in reality the
law enforcement of the world's policeman, of which
the world needs only one. However, as noted, the
world does not generally agree with or appreciate
this position. [327]

It is also common in morality to care what others
think, and it is common around the world to
care what the rest of the world thinks of one's
own country. But it is common within the United
States, not only to reject the golden rule for foreign
relations, [328] but also to simply not care what the
rest of the world thinks. Occasionally, a U.S.-based
pollster surveys people in nations allied to the
United States for opinion on the United States, and
gets very mixed results, and -- more to the point --
very little U.S. media coverage.[329] Very rarely do U.S.
policy debates concern themselves with what the
rest of the world might think. And when they do,
the concern is not usually about the U.S. reputation

for following laws or keeping promises, so much as for a bizarre and unique concept called "credibility," which has nothing to do with the ordinary English word "credibility," but rather denotes a willingness to engage in large-scale war-making.[330]

In 2017, CBS asked, "When it comes to how people around the world feel about the United States today, is it more important for people around the world to like the U.S. for its policies, or is it more important for them to respect the U.S. for its military power?" Somewhat encouragingly, perhaps, 49 percent said "like" while 39 percent said "respect."[331] But in how many countries would such a thing even be asked, much less receive 39 percent support? And doesn't this question conflate people around the world with their governments? Do U.S. tourists really meet ordinary people around the world and hope not so much for them to like the United States as for them to respect U.S. military power? I certainly hope not. And what do most Americans think of an impoverished member of an urban gang who hopes not so much for his gang to be liked as for it to be respected for its fire power? Isn't U.S. exceptionalism an exception to even most Americans' sense of morality?

When people in the United States do pay attention to world opinion, it is generally not through careful or humble study, but through projection. Despite every single incident of foreign terrorism in the United States for which the terrorists have offered any motivation being driven by opposition to U.S. militarism,[332] U.S. pundits spread the belief that huge populations of people around the globe hate the United States for its "freedom." This baseless nonsense fuels bigotry and the idea that foreigners are simply irrational. It fuels the habit of relying on baseless nonsense. And it fuels the baseless belief that the United States leads the world in "freedom" -- otherwise how to explain the absence of similar levels of foreign terrorism in countries with greater civil liberties?

A majority in the United States assumes with no investigation that even its most widely reviled actions, such as the 2003 attack on Iraq, are supported around the world.[333] Americans then proceed, as we have seen, to expect gratitude. These attitudes are anchored in ignorance, including ignorance of both the present and of history. A selective knowledge of history that creates the story of a benevolent world superhero arising out of a reluctant victorious smiting of evil in the cauldron of World War II -- a war entered into to rescue the innocent from death and imperialism -- this sort of knowledge constructed in blissful independence from facts not only far outpaces all recent incidents of "fake news," but does indeed do harm to others.

FLAG WORSHIP

I recently spoke in a forum at a large private high school called Saint Mary's Hall in San Antonio "Military City USA" Texas (the Alamo city's official full name). The topic was the take-a-knee protests of football players and others kneeling during the playing of the U.S. national anthem as a protest against police killings and in support of the black-lives-matter movement. At the beginning of the event, I was one of five speakers on stage, and the moderator asked everyone to stand for the national anthem and pledge of allegiance. Out of everyone on stage and hundreds of students and teachers in the auditorium, I found myself alone in taking a knee.

When I objected, in my remarks, to the practice of pledging allegiance to a flag, the moderator demanded to know what horrible thoughts I believed each student in the room had been thinking when they had pledged allegiance. I replied that part of what was wrong with such rituals was that they involved no thought at all, just mindless repetition.

But the problem with pledging allegiance to a flag, is that someone can wave that flag at you and tell you to do something you might otherwise know better than to do. I can hardly make this point better than was done in the satirical newspaper *The Onion* in its article "U.S. Flag Recalled After Causing 143 Million Deaths."[334] The article began:

WASHINGTON—Citing a series of fatal malfunctions dating back to 1777, flag manufacturer Annin & Company announced Monday that it would be recalling all makes and models of its popular American flag from both foreign and domestic markets. Representatives from the nation's leading flag producer claimed that as many as 143 million deaths in the past two centuries can be attributed directly to the faulty U.S. models, which have been utilized extensively since the 18th century in sectors as diverse as government, the military, and public education.

The following were my opening remarks in San Antonio on March 1, 2018. I have placed video of the full event, which involved a very productive discussion, on my website at davidswanson.org.[335]

Thank you for inviting me. What I contended in the article that got me invited here was that one of the biggest taboos in the United States, one of the behaviors treated most as a heresy, as a violation of national religion, is disrespect for the U.S. flag, the national anthem, and the patriotic militarist exceptionalism that accompany those icons.

We've just seen a school shooting in Florida by a young man trained to shoot by the U.S. Army in the very school where he killed his classmates[336], and you will find virtual silence on that fact, and the silence is self-imposed. Veterans are over twice as likely, statistically, to be mass shooters, and you will not read that in any newspaper.[337] (And, needless to say, it is not somehow grounds for engaging in bigotry toward veterans or for foregoing obvious solutions like banning guns.)

Progressive multi-issue activist coalitions are formed constantly in this country, the Climate March[338], the Women's March[339], etc., and although the military is the top consumer of petroleum[340], although it sucks down 60% of the funding that Congress votes on[341], although it endangers us[342], erodes our liberties[343], and militarizes our police and our schools[344], it goes unmentioned. Foreign policy is unquestionable. Socialism includes no internationalism today.

So, there's something very remarkable about demonstrating against racist police violence by departing from the mandatory body position during the national anthem. It garners attention because it is so very unusual.

And this is uniquely American. Many other countries reserve flags and anthems for international competitions and major occasions, not every adult or child sporting event. In much of the world if you even see any flag, you can ignore it without being suspended from school or shut out of your sports career. Kids have been suspended from U.S. schools for taking a knee as well as for refusing to pledge allegiance[345], Colin Kaepernick is unemployed, the U.S. President wants those who take a knee fired for "disrespecting our flag."[346] And that's a step up from the Alabama Pastor who says anyone who takes a knee should be shot. [347] (But the U.S. Vice President feels entitled to refuse to stand for a flag of Korean unity, despite the obvious passion for it of tens of thousands of people around him.[348])

Flag Day was created by President Woodrow Wilson on the birthday of the U.S. Army during the propaganda campaign for World War I. To my knowledge in only two countries do children regularly recite a pledge to a flag. The original stiff-arm salute they made in the U.S. was changed to a hand on the heart after a straight arm became associated with Nazism.[349] Nowadays, visitors from abroad are often shocked to see U.S. children instructed to stand and robotically chant an oath of obedience to a piece of colored cloth.[350]

U.S. families who lose a loved one in war are presented with a flag instead. A majority of Americans supports criminalizing the burning of a U.S. flag.[351] The U.S. flag appears on Catholic altars in some states, as well as in other churches and sacred arenas.

Texas, with its own national war-making history, may be an exception, but for the most part people do not treat local or state or United Nations or world flags as sacred. It is exclusively the flag that accompanies a military that must be worshiped — a military that pays the National Football League millions of public dollars to perform pro-military ceremonies. [352]

At least some of the players taking a knee will certainly tell you they love the flag (and the troops, and the wars). I have absolutely no interest in pretending to speak for them. They speak very well for themselves. But I am appreciative, whether they like it or not, of their willingness to protest racism by challenging flag worship. I think this is a benefit to both freedom of speech and freedom of religion. After all, freedom of religion rests fundamentally on the ability to refrain from engaging in sacred rituals.[353]

Have you listened carefully to, or read the full lyrics to the U.S. national anthem? The third verse celebrates killing people who had just escaped from slavery.[354] An earlier version had celebrated killing Muslims.[355] The lyricist himself, Francis Scott Key, owned people as slaves and supported lawless police killings of African Americans.[356] Strip the song down to its first verse, and it remains a celebration of war, of the mass killing of human beings, of a war of conquest that failed to take over Canada and instead got the White House burned.[357] And during the course of that valorous piece of blood-soaked stupidity, Key witnessed a battle in which human beings died but a flag survived. And I'm supposed to stand, like an obedient mindless robot, and worship that glorious incident, and it's supposed to matter what I do with my hand, but not what I do with my brain?

I take that back. I'm expected to switch my brain to low-power mode in order to take seriously claims to the effect that militarism protects my freedom, and that I should therefore give up some of my freedom for it. Before the U.S. attacked Iraq in 2003, the CIA said that the only scenario in which Iraq was likely to use any of its vast new stockpiles of "weapons of mass destruction" was if Iraq was attacked.[358] Apart from the nonexistence of the weapons, that was right. The same applies to North Korea. But if North Korea were able to and did launch a missile at the United States, that would still not constitute a threat to your freedoms in particular. It would be a threat to your life. With the age of conquest and colonization gone for three-quarters of a century, and with numbers suggesting that North Korea might need more than its entire population in order to occupy the United States,[359] the chance that North Korea is a threat to your freedom is exactly zero.

But the bombing of Iraq, Afghanistan, Syria, Yemen, Somalia, Pakistan, and Libya, and the threats to North Korea are generating a lot more enemies than they kill.[360] So the threat to your life is real, although the threat to your life posed by automobiles, toddlers with guns, and dozens of other dangers is greater.[361] And the militarism strips away freedoms in the name of protecting them. Recent wars have brought us warrantless surveillance, drones in the skies, lawless imprisonment, mass deportations, expanded government secrecy, whistleblowers imprisoned, public demonstrations contained in cages, metal detectors and cameras everywhere, inauguration protesters facing felony charges[362], and various powers moved from Congress to the White House.[363]

A couple of weeks ago I did a public debate with a professor of ethics from West Point on whether war is ever justifiable. The video is at davidswanson dot org.[364] I argued that not only can no war possibly meet the criteria of just war theory[365], but if one war could, it would have to do so much good as to outweigh all the damage done by keeping the institution of war around, including the risk of nuclear apocalypse, and including the death and suffering far greater than in all the wars created by the diversion of resources away from human and environmental needs. Three percent of U.S. military spending, for example, could end starvation globally.[366] While I don't get enough minutes to make the case for war abolition here, I bring it up to make the following point.

If you view war as an outdated institution, then you want to help everyone engaged in it to transition out of it. Did you know that the U.S. is the only nation on earth that has not ratified the Convention on the Rights of the Child which forbids the military recruitment of children, and that the U.S. military describes the JROTC, as in that school in Florida, as a recruitment program?[367]

The propaganda technique of claiming that if you oppose a war you favor the other side in the war, and that if you oppose flag worship you hate the troops who make up the U.S. military, falls apart when you oppose all war making, and when you support only those enemies in the eyes of the Pentagon that threaten rather than boost its recruitment, namely: free college, free healthcare, good schools, and the general social benefits available to countries that don't dump their treasuries into militarism. Mine are not the positions of a traitor, an insult I'm not fond of. Nor are they the positions of a so-called true patriot, a compliment I'm also not fond of. Patriotism is a problem. We don't need to make America great or declare it already great; we need to recognize the greatness of our own entire and many other species on this fragile little planet.

Kaepernick said, "I am not going to stand up to show pride in a flag for a country that oppresses black people and people of color."[368] Of course, a country has millions of flaws and of achievements. I propose not feeling pride or shame or identifying with a country or national government at all. I propose identifying with humanity and with smaller communities.

I also propose taking notice of the fact that the United States now bombs several nations at a time, none of which contain primarily people labeled "white." "Why should they ask me," said Muhammed Ali, "to put on a uniform and go 10,000 miles from home and drop bombs and bullets on brown people in Vietnam while so-called Negro people in Louisville are treated like dogs and denied simple human rights?"[369]

Why should they ask you even if people in Louisville were treated well? Protesting racist violence but not militarism is a million miles better than nothing. But it is still a major failure to protest racist violence.

Dr. King said we needed to take on racism, militarism, and extreme materialism together. [370] He told the truth.

In a lyric that was sung at the Olympic opening ceremony, John Lennon advised: Imagine there are no countries. It isn't hard to do.[371] He lied. For most people it is very hard to do. But it is something we very badly need to work on.

(For how the above remarks were received, watch the video.[372])

IV. Curing This Disease

The truth sets free only those who build on the truth until it becomes broad enough and solid enough to climb atop it and leap over the prison walls. Exceptionalism is perfectly capable of withstanding the facts presented in the first part of this book and the scornful presentation of the second part of this book. (If the United States is not the greatest in some category, then that's not an important category. If exceptionalists heretofore have engaged in bad behaviors, what we need is a new, more refined exceptionalism. Nationalism is bad, but patriotism is good, or vice versa.)

But if we take seriously the arguments of the third part of this book, that exceptionalism, by its nature, deeply harms the exceptionalists and all those around them -- that it makes us stupider, meaner, and more destructive, or at least blissfully tolerant of public policies that are stupider, meaner, and more destructive -- then we have a responsibility to advance the process of outgrowing exceptionalism.

That means making sure others become aware of what we have learned. And it means taking strategic steps to undo a worldview that harms the world.

HOW WE THINK

Who's "we"? That's the first question. Imagining there're no countries (which is very hard to do) does not mean picking a different country to love or worship. It does not mean switching from loving a country to hating a country. It does not mean replacing arrogance or pride with shame. It does not mean believing national governments don't currently exist. And it does not mean supposing there are not cultural traits that tend to be grouped with your national identity, traits that you may share without even being aware of it.

What it means to me is envisioning the possibility of national governments ceasing to exist, or the easier possibility of national governments losing their prominence in favor of more local and more global decision making. But, more importantly, it means identifying oneself with all of humanity, and with one's local community or communities more strongly than with a national government.

In my town I can know people, I can impact their lives directly, I can take my part in collective decision making, and I can hold affection for the people and places and activities that I know and love. I can do so without any flag or any militarism. Yet I know that my fate is bound up with that of every other person on earth, each of whom is just as valuable as those people I actually know something about. And beyond all of those billions of people are all of the other living things and ecosystems on which our collective future relies. So, I have obvious reasons to think of myself in terms of my locality and my planet, neither of which has very many songs, holidays, or celebratory rituals -- perhaps both should.

Jumping to the scale of the United States is as arbitrary in forming my sense of personal identity as is race or gender. I will no more ever see or know the whole United States than the whole earth. But the whole earth contains people just like me whose futures, and whose descendants' futures are bound up with my own and those of my children. The 4 percent of humanity in the United States has no key interests or futures independent of the other 96 percent. No nation is an island, in the same sense in which no person is an island and any human bell "tolls for thee."[373]

There's no need to be absolutist about this in our thinking, or to work for the actual elimination of nations. Just as one can identify with various groups while still identifying as an individual, just as one can have a family as well as an extended family as well as a neighborhood as well as a club, a sports team, a group of colleagues, and so forth, one can be a human and an American, and the latter both in the sense of belonging to the Western hemisphere and in the sense of belonging to the United States. And people who spend or have spent their lives in multiple nations can identify with multiple nations as well as with humanity and localities and so forth. What I mean to speak to here is primarily a question of emphasis. What or whom do you identify with first? And can you scale your nationalist identity back to something manageable, something that doesn't separate, exclude, or scorn?

Try this experiment: Imagine that space aliens really come to earth and really have, as I think is very unlikely, developed the ability to travel to earth while simultaneously remaining so primitive as to violently attack the places they visit. In contrast to the space aliens, could you identify as an earthling to such an extent as to diminish your other senses of identity? "Earthlings -- F--- Yeah!" "We're Number 1!" "Greatest Earthlings on Earth!" And can you hold that thought, in the absence of the space aliens, and rid yourself of any notion of opposing any other or foreign group, while still holding that earthling thought? Alternatively, can you cast climate change and environmental collapse in the role of the evil alien Hollywood monster against whom humanity must unite?

Or try this one: Imagine that various species of

humans survived to the current day, so that we Sapiens share the earth with the Neanderthals, the Erectus, the tiny little Floresiensis, etc.[374] Could you form your identity in your mind as a Sapiens? And then, can you hold that thought while either imagining the other species back out of existence or imagining learning to be as respectful and kind to the other species of humans as we should perhaps actually be attempting to be to other types of living human and non-human earthlings right now?

As part of diminishing our identity as "Americans," I propose dropping the pretense that being an American is a matter of choosing to think democratically. Not only are other nations, as we have seen, more democratic, but the concept of "un-American" does far more damage than this concept of "American" does good. The availability of "un-American" as a mindless accusation against public policies, political ideologies, public figures, immigrants, sexual preferences, healthcare, secure retirement, gun control, zoning laws, labor unions, and hundreds of other things should be ended. Huge mountains of terrific ideas have been significantly contributed to by Americans, but hardly independently of the rest of the world. The notion that one becomes "American" by holding proper thoughts is inaccurate, exceptionalist, and dangerous, despite the best of intentions on the part of many who advance the idea.

We need a conception of the United States that's closer in several ways to a common conception of your local county or city. It's a legal entity with a certain jurisdiction. It's open to learning from as well as teaching other similar entities. It's unique in cultural ways but cooperative and non-interfering in public policy. It's aware that others will choose to learn from its accomplishments when they are offered respectfully and when actually requested. It's aware that lawful conduct tends to benefit itself and others. Elected leaders of your locality are in most cases, I hope, unlikely to follow President Trump's example in referring to other surrounding jurisdictions as "shitholes" or "shithouses."[375]

Perhaps the most powerful tool for altering habits of thought about groups of people is role reversal. Let's imagine that for whatever reasons, beginning some seventy years ago North Korea drew a line through the United States, from sea to shining sea, and divided it, and educated and trained and armed a brutal dictator in the South United States, and destroyed 80 percent of the cities in the North United States, and killed millions of North USians. Then North Korea refused to allow any U.S. reunification or official end to the war, maintained wartime control of the South United States military, built major North Korean military bases in the South United States, placed missiles just south of the U.S. demilitarized zone that ran through the middle of the country, and imposed brutal economic sanctions on the North United States for decades. As a resident of the North United States, what might you think when the president of North Korea threatened your country with "fire and fury"?[376] Your own government might have gazillions of current and historical crimes and shortcomings to its credit, but what would you think of threats coming from the country that killed your grandparents and walled you off from your cousins? Or would you be too scared to think rationally?

This experiment is possible in hundreds of variations, and I recommend trying it repeatedly in your own mind and in groups, so that people's creativity can feed into the imagination of others. Imagine that you're from the Marshall Islands seeking restitution for nuclear testing and/or the rising seas.[377] Imagine you're from Niger and less than amused that Americans first hear about your country when their government pretends that Iraq purchased uranium in your country, and that Americans only learn about their own military's actions in your country when the U.S. president is rude to the mother of a deceased U.S. soldier.[378] Imagine you're my friends from Vicenza, Italy, who found local and national majority support for blocking the proposed construction of a U.S. Army base but couldn't stop it -- or similar people in Okinawa or Jeju Island or elsewhere around the globe.

And don't just imagine you're the other people.

Learn and then re-tell the stories with all the details inverted. It's not Okinawa. It's Alabama. Japan is filling Alabama with Japanese military bases. The towns and state are opposed, but craven politicians in Washington, D.C., are going along. The military airplane crashes happen in Alabama. The spread of prostitution and drugs happens in Alabama. The local girls raped and murdered are Alabaman. The Japanese troops say it's for your own good whether you think so or not, and they don't really care what you think. You get the idea. This can be done with wealth distribution, with environmental impact, with militarism, with any issue under the sun. The danger of over-simplification should be resisted. The idea is not to stupidly convince yourself that all Americans are 100% evil while all Japanese are some sort of angels. The idea is to reverse some key facts and see whether anything happens to your attitudes. If not, then perhaps your attitudes were fair and respectful to begin with.

Another nominee for most powerful tool for altering habits of thought about groups of people is what goes by the very odd name "humanization." This is the process wherein you supposedly take a human being or group of human beings, and by learning their names and facial expressions and little idiosyncrasies, you "humanize" them, and you come to the conclusion that these humans are . . . wait for it . . . wait for it . . . *humans*. Now, I'm 100 percent in favor of this to whatever extent it is needed and works. I think Americans (and probably most people) should read more foreign books, learn more foreign languages, watch more foreign films, and travel more in ways that truly involve them in foreign cultures. I think students should be required to spend a year as exchange students in foreign families and schools. I think a key test of childhood education in the United States should be: What have these children learned about all of humanity, including the 96% outside the United States?

I am hopeful that at some point we can jump the humanization and arrive squarely on the understanding that, in fact, humans are all humans, whether we know anything about them or not! It might help to pretend that all Hollywood movies have been made about and starring Syrians (or any other nationality). If that were so, if every favorite character from every film and TV show were Syrian, would anyone in the world have any doubt that Syrians were human beings? And what effect would that have on our perception of the reported Israeli government position, seemingly abetted by U.S. government policy, that the best outcome in Syria is for nobody to win but the war to continue forever?[379]

As we learn to think without exceptionalism, we should lose some paranoia. We should rank dangers in their actual order rather than bumping those involving nationally designated enemies to the top. This means finding heart disease, cancer, respiratory disease, automobile accidents, Alzheimer's, diabetes, influenza, pneumonia, kidney disease,[380] and by extension such factors as bad diet, low exercise, unsafe roads, lax gun laws, and lots and lots of other dangers to be scarier than foreign Muslim terrorists or North Korean or Russian politicians.

In fact, I think we should move toward losing the concept of enemy, not just reducing its importance. Someone threatening a crime is a potential criminal, with legitimate or illegitimate grievances, or some of each. The proper question is how to de-escalate any conflict, not how to destroy the enemy. The destruction always destroys primarily ordinary people who had little or nothing to do with the conflict. Once we lose the concept of "enemy," the U.S. government loses any excuse to unconstitutionally spy on us without warrants and violate our other rights. That's when we really might have a chance to expand the freedoms for which nobody has ever hated us.

Moving beyond exceptionalism includes moving beyond the Pinkerist notion that war is what nations other than the United States do, and that therefore war is rapidly disappearing from the earth.[381] And it means rejecting the happy notion that the mass extinction of other species isn't really anything to worry about. A truly unexceptionalist attitude, I think, would recommend to most people figuring out as quickly as possible how to live sustainably on this planet. In contrast, I see a certain affinity between exceptionalist and elitist attitudes and the prioritization of technological solutions to human crises. The notions that you can fix the climate by altering the weather[382], or overcome human failings by merging multiple minds into a new cyborgian being, or even advance human development by littering outerspace with an electric car sent up by rocket ship[383] rely on a level of arrogance that characterizes exceptionalism, and exceptionalistically evade the necessity of forming a human identity and learning to live on earth.

HOW WE TALK

My own town happens to be Charlottesville, Virginia, where in August 2017, a group of fascists mostly from outside of Charlottesville held a hateful and armed rally that made news around the world. The *Washington Post's* Karen Attiah wrote up a report, quoting fictional experts and written in the style in which the *Post* or any other U.S. media outlet might have reported on Charlottesville were it located in some other country, especially a non-Western country or a Pentagon-targeted country:[384]

> The international community is yet again sounding the alarm on ethnic violence in the United States under the new regime of President Trump. The latest flash point occurred this past weekend when the former Confederate stronghold of Charlottesville descended into chaos following rallies of white supremacist groups protesting the removal of statues celebrating leaders of the defeated Confederate states. The chaos turned deadly when Heather Heyer, a member of the white ethnic majority who attended the rally as a counterprotester, was killed when a man with neo-Nazi sympathies allegedly drove his car into a crowd. . . . Experts are also linking the weekend violence to the scourge of domestic terrorism carried out by white males, who have carried out almost twice as many mass attacks on American soil than Muslims have

in recent years. "This is the time for moderates across the white male world to come out and denounce violent racial terrorism, white supremacy and regressive tribal politics," said James Charlotin, a Canadian national security expert. "Why haven't they spoken out?"[385]

There's no real difference between an "administration" and a "regime," or a "demographic" and an "ethnic group," but it sounds as if there is. Asking the world's white males to denounce a fascist rally in Virginia is not crazier than asking the world's Muslims to all denounce the crimes of September 11, 2001, but it sounds as if it is.

The same *Washington Post* editor wrote in the same style following a mass-shooting in Las Vegas:[386]

This week international analysts are sounding the alarm on the increasing instability of the United States after an outbreak of gun violence, government corruption scandals and failure to provide basic services to citizens. In the western

American province of Nevada, nearly 60 people were killed and more than 500 others wounded when a gunman opened fire at a country music festival. The gunman, who killed himself, had 47 guns[387] in his homes and hotel room, along with 50 pounds of explosives and 1,600 rounds of ammunition[388] in his car. "It's mind-boggling that the United States refuses to deal with its gun violence problem," said Jack Harrison, an Australian lawyer. "We managed to ban these type of deadly weapons. After dead children at Sandy Hook and murdered concertgoers in Las Vegas, Americans are showing the world they are willing to sacrifice their fellow citizens on the altar of some fuzzy idea of freedom." Tim Fischer, the former deputy prime minister of Australia who helped implement changes to the nation's gun laws, has even advised[389] Australians against unnecessary travel to the violence-stricken former British colony.

That last sentence was not fiction. Tim Fischer did advise that.

The United States may be no more unstable than some country that its military hopes to soon overthrow, but it's easy enough to depict it as such. The people of the United States haven't actually voted to sacrifice their children to the NRA, but it's simple enough to suggest as much if one builds in the assumption of public influence on government policy. As we have seen above, the U.S. public has very little influence on U.S. national policies.

Is it possible that we are not in the habit of speaking or writing fairly and respectfully about 96 percent of humanity? It's more than possible. But some bits of humanity get better treatment than others. When European journalists are killed in wars, apologies are extended. When a mass-shooting happens in France, "We are all France!" But we are never all Lebanon or Syria or Iraq for some reason. In 2002-2003 the U.S. media claimed that Iraq possessed "weapons of mass destruction," while 3 percent of the voices on network U.S. newscasts opposed the push toward war.[390] But there was never any doubt, nor any discussion of the fact, that the United States itself possessed in great quantities all of the weapons it accused Iraq of possessing[391] (and had in the past helped supply Iraq with some of the weapons it no longer had).[392] I hope it's unnecessary to spell out that the point is not that the United States should have been bombed and occupied, but rather that Iraq should not have been.

Imagine if Iraq had bombed and occupied the United States, something it of course had no interest in doing or ability to do. Here's one thing that would have been rather low on my list of concerns: was the war properly authorized by the Iraqi parliament? How could any legislative procedure in Baghdad possibly legalize bombing my house in the United States? A crime is a crime is a crime, right?

But listen to how Congress members and many others in the United States talk about the legality of war. If only Congress would properly declare wars, they'd be made legal! If you speak like that, you just might be an exceptionalist.

Listen to how advocates on almost any issue in the United States talk about the reforms they want enacted. From food waste to gun control to prisons, people demand that the United States "lead" the world, show "leadership," and be a "leader." This is ridiculous. The United States should *FOLLOW* the rest of the world and work hard to lift itself up. If you talk as though the United States must always be the leader, you just might be an exceptionalist.

Listen hard in U.S. culture for any processes of reform, development, evolution, or progress that are built on admitting past mistakes and attempting something better. The degree to which mainstream German culture teaches and tries to overcome past German mistakes and crimes is greatly to its credit. The degree to which mainstream U.S. culture teaches and tries to overcome past German crimes is a little bit less to its credit. Who's going to teach and overcome past U.S. mistakes and crimes? If you don't acknowledge U.S. mistakes and world-class crimes, you just might be an exceptionalist.

HOW WE ACT

Whether "we" sought world dominance or were dragged reluctantly into a trillion-dollar-a-year empire (like Dick Cheney being hauled against his will into a Vice Presidential nomination), must the U.S. government desperately cling to it now? Is the longstanding straw man of "isolationism" the only other choice? Or is another course available that could benefit the people of the United States and of the world?

While the United States is quite far from being a leader on many issues, it can exercise enormous influence on any issue it chooses. Were it to add its weight, respectfully and cooperatively, on the environment or disarmament or an expansion of human rights, the global impact might be larger than we can easily imagine.

Let's not fall into the familiar but ridiculous trap of supposing that there is only a choice between militarily occupying a country and "abandoning" it. Iranian Nobel Peace Prize Laureate Shirin Ebadi proposed that the United States not attack Afghanistan but rather build a school in Afghanistan in the name of each victim of September 11, 2001. Who at this point can argue, after almost 16.5 years of war, that Ebadi's plan would have been worse? It would likely have resulted in far more people in Afghanistan learning what happened on September 11th.

I remember the debate in 2013 over whether President Barack Obama, Secretary of State John Kerry, and gang should heavily bomb Syria.[393] There were people on the "left" telling me that if we cared about and valued Syrians we would bomb them, that they were just as worthy of being bombed as anyone else. There were people on the "right" telling me that no matter how much we bombed the Syrians, they would never be properly grateful for it, so we really shouldn't bother, what we needed were tax cuts. Yet others on the "left" said good American dollars shouldn't be wasted on bombing Syrians, but should be spent on good old Americans right "here at home." This, of course, set off choruses of opposition to greed and xenophobia from the first group, those wanting to bomb Syrians out of the goodness of their hearts.

Needless to say, I think the foregoing is the wrong debate for a number of reasons. How would it sound as a Syrian debate over whether to bomb Maryland? I'm serious. Re-write it with lots of details, set in Syria, as a debate over whether to bomb specific "strategic" locations in Maryland. If, after doing that, something doesn't strike you as wrong about it, perhaps you're not suffering from exceptionalism but from an overriding love of bombs. It's hard for me to diagnose that condition from a distance. And the only disease I'm hoping to cure with this book is exceptionalism.

If we become humans first, if we deemphasize national competition, we will have a different perspective on environmental policy (the chief point becoming saving the earth, not sticking it to the poor nations and the Chinese), on war policy (the chief point being to avoid it), on economic policy (the main goal becoming the well-being of all, not the hoarding of loot), and of course on immigration policy. We might even stop forcing new U.S. citizens to swear that they abandon all allegiance to anywhere else and to promise to fight in U.S. wars, as is currently done in the process of "naturalizing" new citizens.[394]

As a step toward thinking of oneself as a world citizen I recommend that people pick up world passports.[395] As regards the horrifying bogeyman of "world government," I recommend the following:

1. much more power moved from national and state to local government;
2. more power moved from national to state government;
3. a much smaller U.S. government that invests far more in all areas of human and environmental needs (accomplishing this miracle by slashing military spending);
4. a democratically reformed or replaced United

Nations with no armed forces, and no special privileges for five nations currently permanent members of the Security Council;

5. democratically   reformed   or   replaced international courts of justice and crime;

6. appropriate oversight where needed of lower levels of government by higher, and vice versa.

I have drafted and will soon publish a plan for a better system of world law and governance. But any system is only as good as the thinking and habits of the people in it. The larger a project, the greater the dangers of abuse and corruption. No project as big as the world stands a chance if the wealthiest, most heavily armed nation in the world believes itself to be an exception to all rules and entitled to enforce its exceptionality at enormous cost to itself and others.

Should the world boycott, divest, and sanction the United States? I don't know. I hardly think it's my place to advise the world to kick a rhinoceros I'm sitting on. I do advise beginning with the gentlest but firmest of approaches.

I am, however, happy to advise that those of us within the United States -- with any help and advice we can get from others -- should proceed with the project of this book, much of which will involve ceasing to be just people within the United States and becoming part of the planet's people who take on the project of protecting the planet as a collective group effort in which we can all win or lose together.

Acknowledgements

Thanks to the thousands of people I've learned from. Thanks to my loving family. Thanks to those who rapidly gave me some helpful feedback on the book in the three days between when I wrote it and when I finalized it for publication, including Jeff Cohen, Mike Ferner, Marc Eliot Stein, Linda Swanson, Pat Elder, and Robert Fantina. Thanks to Pexels.com for the free image used on the cover.[396] Thanks to my two employers, World Beyond War and RootsAction.org, for allowing me 1 week away from other work. I wrote the vast bulk of this book in 5 days in March 2018. If you'd like to see what sort of book I could write if I had 2 or more weeks, please donate at davidswanson.org.

About the Author

David Swanson is an author, activist, journalist, and radio host. He is the director of World Beyond War, a global nonviolent movement to end war and establish a just and sustainable peace. He is campaign coordinator for RootsAction.org.

David's books include *War Is A Lie* (a catalog of the types of falsehoods told about wars), *War Is Never Just* (a refutation of just war theory), and *When the World Outlawed War* (an account of the 1920s peace movement), as well as (co-author) *A Global Security System: An Alternative to War* (a vision of a world of nonviolent institutions).

David blogs at DavidSwanson.org and WarIsACrime. org. He hosts a weekly radio show called Talk Nation Radio. He speaks frequently on the topic of war and peace, and engages in all kinds of nonviolent activism. David holds a Master's degree in philosophy from UVA and has long lived and worked in Charlottesville, Virginia.

End Notes

The website addresses in the following end notes were all accessed on March 16, 2018.

1   —"List of Countries by Area," Wikipedia, https://simple.wikipedia.org/wiki/List_of_countries_by_area
—"List of Countries and Dependencies by Area," Wikipedia, https://en.wikipedia.org/wiki/List_of_countries_and_dependencies_by_area.
—"Geography > Land Area > Square Miles: Countries Compared," Nation Master, http://www.nationmaster.com/country-info/stats/Geography/Land-area/Square-miles#.
—"Countries of the World by Area," One World Nations Online, http://www.nationsonline.org/oneworld/countries_by_area.htm.

2   —"List of Countries by Population (United Nations)," *Wikipedia*, https://en.wikipedia.org/wiki/List_of_countries_by_population_(United_Nations).
—"List of Countries and Dependencies by Population," *Wikipedia*, https://en.wikipedia.org/wiki/List_of_countries_and_dependencies_by_population.
—"Countries in the World by Population (2018)," *Worldometers*, http://www.worldometers.info/world-population/population-by-country.
—"Countries of the World Ordered by Population Size," *List of Countries of the World*, http://www.listofcountriesoftheworld.com/population.html.

3   "The Legatum Prosperity Index 2017,"

Legatum Institute, https://lif.blob.core.windows.
net/lif/docs/default-source/default-library/
pdf55f152ff15736886a8b2ff00001f4427.pdf?sfvrsn=0.

4   Ian Vasquez and Tanja Porcnik, "The Human
Freedom Index 2017," *the Cato Institute, the Fraser
Institute, and the Friedrich Naumann Foundation for
Freedom*, https://object.cato.org/sites/cato.org/files/
human-freedom-index-files/2017-human-freedom-
index-2.pdf.

5   "2017 World Freedom Index," http://www.
worldfreedomindex.com.

6   "Civil Liberties," *World Audit*, http://www.
worldaudit.org/civillibs.htm.

7   "Ranking 2017," *Reporters Without Borders*,
https://rsf.org/en/ranking/2017.

8   "2018 Index of Economic Freedom," *The
Heritage Foundation*, https://www.heritage.org/index/
country/unitedstates.

9   "World Index of Moral Freedom," *Wikipedia*,
https://en.wikipedia.org/wiki/World_Index_of_Moral_
Freedom.

10   "Democracy Index," *Wikipedia*, https://
en.wikipedia.org/wiki/Democracy_Index.

11   "Polity Data Series," *Wikipedia*, https://
en.wikipedia.org/wiki/Polity_data_series.

12   —Michelle Ye Hee Lee, "Yes, U.S. Locks People Up at a Higher Rate Than Any Other Country," *Washington Post*, https://www.washingtonpost.com/news/fact-checker/wp/2015/07/07/yes-u-s-locks-people-up-at-a-higher-rate-than-any-other-country/?utm_term=.5ea21d773e21 (July 7, 2015). —"List of Countries by Incarceration Rate," *Wikipedia*, https://en.wikipedia.org/wiki/List_of_countries_by_incarceration_rate.

13   "Top Countries Having More PhDs in World," *The Educationist*, http://educationist.com.pk/report-top-countries-having-more-phds-in-world.

14   Kevin Sullivan and Mary Jordan, "Elitists, Crybabies and Junky Degrees," *Washington Post*, http://www.washingtonpost.com/sf/national/2017/11/25/elitists-crybabies-and-junky-degrees/?tid=sm_fb&utm_term=.0f8160048a27 (November 25, 2017).

15   "Best Global Universities Rankings," *U.S. News & World Report*, https://www.usnews.com/education/best-global-universities/rankings?page=10

16   "World University Rankings 2018," *Times Higher Education*, https://www.timeshighereducation.com/world-university-rankings/2018/world-ranking#!/page/0/length/25/sort_by/rank/sort_order/asc/cols/stats.

17   Academy Ranking of World Universities, http://shanghairanking.com/ARWU2017.html.

18   Kelsey Sheehy, "Undergraduates Around the

World Face Student Loan Debt, *U.S. News & World Report*, https://www.usnews.com/education/best-global-universities/articles/2013/11/13/undergrads-around-the-world-face-student-loan-debt (November 13, 2013).

19   —"College Access and Affordability: USA vs. the World," *Value Colleges*, https://www.valuecolleges.com/collegecosts.
—"List of Countries by Tertiary Education Attainment," *Wikipedia*, https://en.wikipedia.org/wiki/List_of_countries_by_tertiary_education_attainment.

20   —Drew Desliver, "U.S. Students Academic Achievement Still Lags That of Their Peers in Many Other Countries," *Pew Research Center*, http://www.pewresearch.org/fact-tank/2017/02/15/u-s-students-internationally-math-science (February 15, 2017).
—"Reading Literacy: Average Scores," *National Center for Education Statistics*, http://nces.ed.gov/surveys/pisa/pisa2012/pisa2012highlights_5a.asp.

21   "Trends in International Mathematics and Science Study," *Wikipedia*, https://en.wikipedia.org/wiki/Trends_in_International_Mathematics_and_Science_Study.

22   "All-Time Olympic Games Medal Table," *Wikipedia*, https://en.wikipedia.org/wiki/All-time_Olympic_Games_medal_table.

23   "2018 Winter Olympics Medal Tracker," *ESPN*, http://www.espn.com/olympics/winter/2018/medals.

24   "List of Countries by GDP (Nominal)," *Wikipedia*,

https://en.wikipedia.org/wiki/List_of_countries_by_
GDP_(nominal).

25   "List of Countries by GDP (PPP)," *Wikipedia*,
https://en.wikipedia.org/wiki/List_of_countries_by_
GDP_(PPP).

26   "List of Countries by GDP (Nominal Per Capita),"
Wikipedia, https://en.wikipedia.org/wiki/List_of_
countries_by_GDP_ percent28nominal percent29_per_
capita.

27   "List of Countries by the Number of Billionaires,"
Wikipedia, https://en.wikipedia.org/wiki/List_of_
countries_by_the_number_of_billionaires.

28   —Elise Gould and Hilary Wething, "U.S. Poverty
Rates Higher, Safety Net Weaker Than in Peer Countries,"
Economic Policy Institute, http://www.epi.org/
publication/ib339-us-poverty-higher-safety-net-weaker
(July 24, 2012).
—Max Fisher, "Map: How 35 Countries Compare on Child
Poverty (the U.S. Is Ranked 34th),: *Washington Post*,
https://www.washingtonpost.com/news/worldviews/
wp/2013/04/15/map-how-35-countries-compare-
on-child-poverty-the-u-s-is-ranked-34th/?utm_term=.
a3b0797b716e (April 15, 2013).
—Christopher Ingraham, "Child Poverty in the U.S. Is
Among the Worst in the Developed World," *Washington
Post*, https://www.washingtonpost.com/news/
wonk/wp/2014/10/29/child-poverty-in-the-u-s-
is-among-the-worst-in-the-developed-world/?utm_
term=.217ecc2c90ee (October 29, 2014).
—"Measuring Child Poverty," *UNICEF*, https://www.

unicef-irc.org/publications/pdf/rc10_eng.pdf (May 2012).

29   "The World Fact Book: Country Comparison: Distribution of Family Income: GINI Index," *Central Intelligence Agency*, https://www.cia.gov/library/publications/the-world-factbook/rankorder/2172rank.html.

30   "GINI Index (World Bank Estimate) Country Ranking," *Index Mundi*, https://www.indexmundi.com/facts/indicators/SI.POV.GINI/rankings.

31   "List of Countries by Distribution of Wealth," *Wikipedia*, https://en.wikipedia.org/wiki/List_of_countries_by_distribution_of_wealth.

32   Philip Alston, "Extreme Poverty in America: Read the UN Special Monitor's Report," *The Guardian*, https://www.theguardian.com/world/2017/dec/15/extreme-poverty-america-un-special-monitor-report (December 15, 2017).

33   David Johnson, "These Are the Most Productive Countries in the World," *Time*, http://time.com/4621185/worker-productivity-countries (January 4, 2017).

34   —Elise Gould, "U.S. Lags Behind Peer Countries in Mobility," *Economic Policy Institute*, http://www.epi.org/publication/usa-lags-peer-countries-mobility (October 10, 2012).
—Ben Lorica, "Prosperity and Upward Mobility: U.S. and Other Countries," *Verisi Data Studio*, http://www.

verisi.com/resources/prosperity-upward-mobility.htm
(November 2011).
—Steven Perlberg, "These Two Ladders Perfectly
Illustrate the Evolution of Income Mobility and
Inequality in America," *Business Insider*, http://www.
businessinsider.com/harvard-upward-mobility-
study-2014-1 (January 23, 2014).
—Katie Sanders, "Is it Easier to Obtain the American
Dream in Europe," *Politifact*, http://www.politifact.com/
punditfact/statements/2013/dec/19/steven-rattner/
it-easier-obtain-american-dream-europe (December 19,
2013).

35   "Patent Counts by Country, State, and Year," *U.S.
Patent and Trademark Office*, https://www.uspto.gov/
web/offices/ac/ido/oeip/taf/cst_all.htm (December
2015).

36   —"World Intellectual Property Indicators,"
Wikipedia, https://en.wikipedia.org/wiki/World_
Intellectual_Property_Indicators.
—"Patent Applications, Residents: Country Ranking,"
Index Mundi, https://www.indexmundi.com/facts/
indicators/IP.PAT.RESD/rankings.
—"Ranking of the 10 Countries That Filed the Most
International Patent Applications in 2016," *Statista*,
https://www.statista.com/statistics/256845/ranking-
of-the-10-countries-who-filed-the-most-international-
patent-applications.

37   "World Intellectual Property Indicators,"
Wikipedia, https://en.wikipedia.org/wiki/World_
Intellectual_Property_Indicators.

38   "The Most Litigious Countries in the World," *Clements Worldwide*, https://www.clements.com/sites/default/files/resources/The-Most-Litigious-Countries-in-the-World.pdf.

39   Tomer Zarchin, "Israel First in World for Lawyers per Capita, Study Finds," *Haaretz*, https://www.haaretz.com/1.5039519 (August 3, 2011).

40   "America's Lawyers: Guilty as Charged," *The Economist*, https://www.economist.com/news/leaders/21571141-cheaper-legal-education-and-more-liberal-rules-would-benefit-americas-lawyersand-their (February 2, 2013).

41   —"All Time Worldwide Box Office," *The Numbers*, https://www.the-numbers.com/box-office-records/worldwide/all-movies/cumulative/all-time.
—"List of Highest Grossing Films," *Wikipedia*, https://en.wikipedia.org/wiki/List_of_highest-grossing_films.
—Richard Wike, "American Star Power Still Rules the Globe," *Pew Research Center*, http://www.pewglobal.org/2013/02/22/american-star-power-still-rules-the-globe (February 22, 2013).

42   —"The Top Ten Best Selling Music Singles in the World (2017)," *Top 10 of Anything and Everything*, https://theverybesttop10.com/best-selling-music-singles.
—"List of Best-Selling Music Artists," *Wikipedia*, https://en.wikipedia.org/wiki/List_of_best-selling_music_artists.
—"Best Selling Music Albums," *Top 10 of Anything and Everything*, https://theverybesttop10.com/best-selling-

music-albums.

43   —"List of Best Selling Books," *Wikipedia*, https://
en.wikipedia.org/wiki/List_of_best-selling_books.
—"Top Ten Best Selling Books of All Time in the World,"
Top 101 News, http://top101news.com/2015-2016-
2017-2018/news/education/best-selling-books-all-
time-world.

44   "Best Countries: United States," *U.S. News &
World Report*, https://www.usnews.com/news/best-
countries/united-states.

45   "Soft Power," *Wikipedia*, https://en.wikipedia.
org/wiki/Soft_power.

46   "List of Languages by Total Number of Speakers,"
Wikipedia, https://en.wikipedia.org/wiki/List_of_
languages_by_total_number_of_speakers.

47   Kat Devlin, "Learning a Foreign Language
a 'Must' in Europe, Not So in America," *Pew
Research Center*, http://www.pewresearch.org/fact-
tank/2015/07/13/learning-a-foreign-language-a-must-
in-europe-not-so-in-america (July 13, 2015).

48   "List of Sovereign States and Dependent
Territories by Immigrant Population," *Wikipedia*,
https://en.wikipedia.org/wiki/List_of_sovereign_states_
and_dependent_territories_by_immigrant_population.

49   Amy Sherman, "Does the United States Have
the Highest Number of Immigrants, as Marco Rubio
Says?" *Politifact*, http://www.politifact.com/florida/

statements/2015/may/13/marco-rubio/does-united-states-have-highest-number-immigrants- (May 13, 2015).

50   —Brendan McBryde, "10 Countries That Accept the Most Refugees," *Borgen Magazine*, http://www.borgenmagazine.com/10-countries-that-accept-refugees (January 22, 2016).
—"List of Countries by Refugee Population," *Wikipedia*, https://en.wikipedia.org/wiki/List_of_countries_by_refugee_population.

51   David Cook-Martin and David Scott Fitzgerald, "How Legacies of Racism Persist in U.S. Immigration Policy," *Scholars Strategy Network*, http://www.scholarsstrategynetwork.org/brief/how-legacies-racism-persist-us-immigration-policy (June 2014).

52   "Best Countries for Immigrants," *U.S. News & World Report*, https://www.usnews.com/news/best-countries/immigrants-full-list.

53   Juan Gonzalez, "Harvest of Empire: The Untold Story of Latinos in America," http://harvestofempiremovie.com.

54   —Dana Frank, "In Honduras, A Mess Made in the U.S.," *New York Times*, http://www.nytimes.com/2012/01/27/opinion/in-honduras-a-mess-helped-by-the-us.html (January 26, 2012).
—Karen Attiah, "Hillary Clinton's Dodgy Answers on Honduras Coup," *Washington Post*, https://www.washingtonpost.com/blogs/post-partisan/wp/2016/04/19/hillary-clintons-dodgy-answers-on-

honduras-coup/?utm_term=.392410e13225 (April 19, 2016).

—Tim Shorrock, "How Hillary Clinton Militarized US Policy in Honduras," *The Nation*, https://www.thenation.com/article/how-hillary-clinton-militarized-us-policy-in-honduras (April 5, 2016).

55   Will Oremus, "The USA Is Number One (in Cheese Production)," *Slate*, http://www.slate.com/articles/news_and_politics/politics/2012/07/the_greatest_country_in_the_world_the_usa_is_tops_in_cheese_production_and_these_23_other_categories_.html (July 3, 2012).

56   "List of Countries by Carbon Dioxide Emissions," *Wikipedia*, https://en.wikipedia.org/wiki/List_of_countries_by_carbon_dioxide_emissions

57   Naomi Klein, "Fight Climate Change, Not Wars," *NaomiKlein.org*, http://www.naomiklein.org/articles/2009/12/fight-climate-change-not-wars (December 10, 2009).

58   Melissa Breyer, "Top 10 Countries Killing the Planet," *Care2*, https://www.care2.com/greenliving/top-10-countries-ruining-the-planet.html (May 11, 2010).

59   Corey J. A. Bradshaw, Xingli Giam, Navjot S. Sodhi, "Evaluating the Environmental Impact of Countries," *PLOS One*, http://journals.plos.org/plosone/article?id=10.1371/journal.pone.0010440#pone.0010440.s008 (May 3, 2010).

60   "United States of America," *Happy Planet Index*, https://happyplanetindex.org/countries/united-states-of-america.

61   "2018 EPI Results," *Environmental Performance Index*, https://epi.envirocenter.yale.edu/epi-topline?country=&order=field_epi_rank_new&sort=asc.

62   Danielle Knight, "Climate: U.S. Exempts Military from Kyoto Treaty," *Inter Press Service*, http://www.ipsnews.net/1998/05/climate-us-exempts-military-from-kyoto-treaty (May 20, 1998).

63   Arthur Neslen, "Pentagon to lose emissions exemption under Paris climate deal," *The Guardian*, https://www.theguardian.com/environment/2015/dec/14/pentagon-to-lose-emissions-exemption-under-paris-climate-deal (December 14, 2015).

64   "Paris Agreement - Status of Ratification," *United Nations*, http://unfccc.int/paris_agreement/items/9444.php.

65   Joe Myers, "Foreign aid: These countries are the most generous," *World Economic Forum*, https://www.weforum.org/agenda/2016/08/foreign-aid-these-countries-are-the-most-generous (August 19, 2016).

66   Joe Myers, "Foreign aid: These countries are the most generous," *World Economic Forum*, https://www.weforum.org/agenda/2016/08/foreign-aid-these-countries-are-the-most-generous (August 19, 2016).

67   "List of Development Aid Country Donors,"

Wikipedia, https://en.wikipedia.org/wiki/List_of_
development_aid_country_donors.

68   Max Bearak and Lazaro Gamio, "The U.S. foreign
aid budget, visualized," *Washington Post*, https://www.
washingtonpost.com/graphics/world/which-countries-
get-the-most-foreign-aid (October 18, 2016).

69   Steven Radelet, "Think Again: U.S. Foreign Aid,"
Foreign Policy, https://foreignpolicy.com/2005/03/01/
think-again-u-s-foreign-aid (March 1, 2005).

70   Carol Adelman, Bryan Schwartz & Elias
Riskin, "Index of Global Philanthropy and Remittances
2016," *Hudson Institute*, https://www.hudson.org/
research/13314-index-of-global-philanthropy-and-
remittances-2016 (February 15th, 2017).

71   —"Statistics," *Philanthropy Roundtable*, http://
www.philanthropyroundtable.org/almanac/statistics.
—Global Impact, https://charity.org.

72   "CAF World Giving Index 2016," *Charities Aid
Foundation*, https://www.cafonline.org/docs/default-
source/about-us-publications/1950a_wgi_2016_report_
web_v2_241016.pdf (October 2016).

73   "Statistics," *Philanthropy Roundtable*, http://
www.philanthropyroundtable.org/almanac/statistics.

74   Dylan Matthews, "Only a third of charitable
contributions go to the poor," *Washington Post*,
https://www.washingtonpost.com/news/wonk/
wp/2013/05/30/only-a-third-of-charitable-

contributions-go-the-poor/?utm_term=.b83df0d2f21d
(May 30, 2013).

75   "List of Countries by Life Expectancy," *Wikipedia*,
https://en.wikipedia.org/wiki/List_of_countries_by_life_
expectancy.

76   "List of Countries by Life Expectancy," *Wikipedia*,
https://en.wikipedia.org/wiki/List_of_countries_by_life_
expectancy.

77   "List of Countries by Life Expectancy," *Wikipedia*,
https://en.wikipedia.org/wiki/List_of_countries_by_life_
expectancy.

78   "List of Countries by Life Expectancy," *Wikipedia*,
https://en.wikipedia.org/wiki/List_of_countries_by_life_
expectancy.

79   "List of Countries by Total Health Expenditure
per Capita," *Wikipedia*, https://en.wikipedia.org/wiki/
List_of_countries_by_total_health_expenditure_per_
capita.

80   "Where Do You Get the Most for Your Health
Care Dollar?" *Bloomberg*, http://www.bloomberg.com/
infographics/2014-09-15/most-efficient-health-care-
around-the-world.html (Sept. 18, 2014).

81   Sean Gorman, "Dan Gecker says U.S. only wealthy
nation without universal health care," *Politifact*, http://
www.politifact.com/virginia/statements/2015/sep/01/
dan-gecker/dan-gecker-says-us-only-wealth-nation-
without-univ (September 1st, 2015).

82   "The Global Competitiveness Report 2017–2018,"
World Economic Forum, https://www.weforum.org/
reports/the-global-competitiveness-report-2017-2018
(September 26, 2017).

83   — Rick Noack and Lazaro Gamio, "Map: The best
(and worst) countries to be a mother," *Washington Post*,
https://www.washingtonpost.com/news/worldviews/
wp/2015/05/08/map-the-best-and-worst-countries-
to-be-a-mother/?utm_term=.483da0062489 (May 8,
2015).
—*Save the Children*, http://www.savethechildren.org.

84   "The World Factbook: Country Comparison:
Infant Mortality Rate," *Central Intelligence Agency*,
https://www.cia.gov/library/publications/the-world-
factbook/rankorder/2091rank.html

85   Rick Noack and Lazaro Gamio, "Map: The best
(and worst) countries to be a mother," *Washington Post*,
https://www.washingtonpost.com/news/worldviews/
wp/2015/05/08/map-the-best-and-worst-countries-
to-be-a-mother/?utm_term=.483da0062489 (May 8,
2015).

86   Megan Trimble, "U.S. Kids More Likely to Die
Than Kids in 19 Other Nations," *U.S. News & World
Report*, https://www.usnews.com/news/best-
countries/articles/2018-01-11/us-has-highest-child-
mortality-rate-of-20-rich-countries (Jan. 11, 2018).

87   "Child well-being in rich countries: A
comparative overview," *UNICEF*, https://www.unicef-irc.

org/publications/pdf/rc11_eng.pdf (April 2013).

88   Gretchen Livingston, "Among 41 nations, U.S. is the outlier when it comes to paid parental leave," *Pew Research Center*, http://www.pewresearch.org/fact-tank/2016/09/26/u-s-lacks-mandated-paid-parental-leave (September 26, 2016).

89   "Explore findings from the new report: 'U.S. Health in International Perspectives'," *The National Academies of Sciences, Engineering, Medicine*, http://sites.nationalacademies.org/DBASSE/CPOP/DBASSE_080393#violence.

90   "List of Countries by Intentional Homicide Rate," *Wikipedia*, https://en.wikipedia.org/wiki/List_of_countries_by_intentional_homicide_rate.

91   Erin Grinshteyn, David Hemenway, "Violent Death Rates: The US Compared with Other High-income OECD Countries, 2010," *The American Journal of Medicine*, http://www.amjmed.com/article/S0002-9343(15)01030-X/fulltext (March 2016).

92   "Which are the laziest countries on earth?," *The Guardian*, https://www.theguardian.com/news/datablog/2012/jul/18/physical-inactivity-country-laziest#data.

93   "Average minutes per day spent on sport and exercise in OECD countries plus China, India and South Africa by gender, as of 2016," *Statista*, https://www.statista.com/statistics/522015/time-spent-sports-countries.

94   Amir Khan, "America Tops List of 10 Most Obese Countries," *U.S. News & World Report*, https://health.usnews.com/health-news/health-wellness/articles/2014/05/28/america-tops-list-of-10-most-obese-countries (May 28, 2014).

95   "The Most Obese Countries In The World," *World Atlas*, https://www.worldatlas.com/articles/29-most-obese-countries-in-the-world.html.

96   Oliver Smith, "World Obesity Day: Which countries have the biggest weight problem?," *The Telegraph*, https://www.telegraph.co.uk/travel/maps-and-graphics/the-most-obese-fattest-countries-in-the-world (October 11, 2017).

97   "Report: Obesity Rates by Country – 2017," *Renew Bariatrics*, https://renewbariatrics.com/obesity-rank-by-countries.

98   Ana Swanson, "The U.S. isn't the fattest country in the world – but it's close," *Washington Post*, https://www.washingtonpost.com/news/wonk/wp/2015/04/22/youll-never-guess-the-worlds-fattest-country-and-no-its-not-the-u-s/?utm_term=.535bccee9a54 (April 22, 2015).

99   "World Happiness Report 2017," Editors: John Helliwell, Richard Layard and Jeffrey Sachs, http://worldhappiness.report/wp-content/uploads/sites/2/2017/03/HR17.pdf.

100   "United States of America," Happy Planet Index,

https://happyplanetindex.org/countries/united-states-of-america.

101   "Human Development Index and its components," *United Nations Development Programme*, http://hdr.undp.org/en/composite/HDI.

102   "The Good Country," https://goodcountry.org/index/results.

103   "United States: Global Competitiveness Index 2017-2018 edition," *World Economic Forum*, http://reports.weforum.org/global-competitiveness-index-2017-2018/countryeconomy-profiles/#economy=USA.

104   "List of Countries by Electricity Production from Renewable Sources," *Wikipedia*, https://en.wikipedia.org/wiki/List_of_countries_by_electricity_production_from_renewable_sources.

105   "Democracy Index 2017: Free speech under attack," *The Economist*, http://www.eiu.com/Handlers/WhitepaperHandler.ashx?fi=Democracy_Index_2017.pdf&mode=wp&campaignid=DemocracyIndex2017.

106   "Referendums by Country," *Wikipedia*, https://en.wikipedia.org/wiki/Referendum#Referendums_by_country.

107   Nick Thompson, "International campaign finance: How do countries compare?," *CNN*, https://edition.cnn.com/2012/01/24/world/global-campaign-finance (March 5, 2012).

108   Pippa Norris, "America is no model state: U.S. elections rank worst among Western democracies," *Salon*, https://www.salon.com/2016/04/15/america_is_no_model_democracy_u_s_elections_rank_worst_among_western_states_partner (April 15, 2016).

109   Drew DeSilver, "U.S. trails most developed countries in voter turnout," *Pew Research Center*, http://www.pewresearch.org/fact-tank/2017/05/15/u-s-voter-turnout-trails-most-developed-countries.

110   Martin Gilens and Benjamin I. Page, "Testing Theories of American Politics: Elites, Interest Groups, and Average Citizens," *Perspectives on Politics*, https://www.cambridge.org/core/journals/perspectives-on-politics/article/testing-theories-of-american-politics-elites-interest-groups-and-average-citizens/62327F513959D0A304D4893B382B992B (September 18, 2014).

111   Caroline Bologna, "Here's Why Americans Are So Obsessed With The Royals," *HuffPost*, https://www.huffingtonpost.com/entry/british-royal-family-obsession_us_5a4b0788e4b025f99e1d0a4b (January 12, 2018).

112   David Swanson, "U.S. Wars and Hostile Actions: A List," *Let's Try Democracy*, http://davidswanson.org/warlist.

113   David Swanson, "U.S. Wars and Hostile Actions: A List," *Let's Try Democracy*, http://davidswanson.org/warlist.

114   Scott Shane, "Russia Isn't the Only One Meddling in Elections. We Do It, Too," *New York Times*, https://www.nytimes.com/2018/02/17/sunday-review/russia-isnt-the-only-one-meddling-in-elections-we-do-it-too.html (February 17, 2018).

115   Dov H. Levin, "Partisan electoral interventions by the great powers: Introducing the PEIG Dataset," *SAGE Journals*, http://journals.sagepub.com/doi/abs/10.1177/0738894216661190 (September 19, 2016).

116   Dov H. Levin, "When the Great Power Gets a Vote: The Effects of Great Power Electoral Interventions on Election Results," https://academic.oup.com/isq/article/60/2/189/1750842 (February 13, 2016, Appendix 2).

117   "James Woolsey on the Russians' efforts to disrupt elections," *Fox News*, https://video.foxnews.com/v/5735486561001/?#sp=show-clips (February 16, 2018).

118   "List of Countries by Military Expenditures," *Wikipedia*, https://en.wikipedia.org/wiki/List_of_countries_by_military_expenditures

119   "Trump's FY2019 Budget Request Has Massive Cuts for Nearly Everything But the Military," *National Priorities Project*, https://www.nationalpriorities.org/analysis/2018/trumps-fy2019-budget-request-has-massive-cuts-nearly-everything-military (February 12, 2018).

120   Chris Hellman, "Tomgram: Chris Hellman, $1.2 Trillion for National Security," *TomDispatch*, http://www.tomdispatch.com/blog/175361 (March 1, 2011).

121   "List of Countries by Military Expenditure per Capita," *Wikipedia*, https://en.wikipedia.org/wiki/List_of_countries_by_military_expenditure_per_capita.

122   "List of Countries by Military Expenditures," *Wikipedia*, https://en.wikipedia.org/wiki/List_of_countries_by_military_expenditures.

123   Niall McCarthy, "The World's Biggest Employers [Infographic]," *Forbes*, https://www.forbes.com/sites/niallmccarthy/2015/06/23/the-worlds-biggest-employers-infographic/#5a79fdb2686b (June 23, 2015).

124   David Swanson, "What Are Foreign Military Bases for?," *Let's Try Democracy*, http://davidswanson.org/what-are-foreign-military-bases-for (July 13, 2015).

125   David Swanson, "How Outlawing War Changed the World in 1928," *Let's Try Democracy*, http://davidswanson.org/how-outlawing-war-changed-the-world-in-1928 (September 12, 2017).

126   David Swanson, "What Are Foreign Military Bases for?," *Let's Try Democracy*, http://davidswanson.org/what-are-foreign-military-bases-for (July 13, 2015).

127   "List of Top International Rankings by Country," *Wikipedia*, https://en.wikipedia.org/wiki/List_of_top_international_rankings_by_country.

128   "Mapping Militarism," *World Beyond War*, http://www.worldbeyondwar.org/wp-content/uploads/statplanet/StatPlanet.html.

129   "Mapping Militarism," *World Beyond War*, http://www.worldbeyondwar.org/wp-content/uploads/statplanet/StatPlanet.html.

130   W.J. Hennigan, Brian Bennett and Nabih Bulos, "In Syria, militias armed by the Pentagon fight those armed by the CIA," *Los Angeles Times*, http://www.latimes.com/world/middleeast/la-fg-cia-pentagon-isis-20160327-story.html (March 27, 2016).

131   "War Endangers Us," *World Beyond War*, http://worldbeyondwar.org/endangers.

132   "War Erodes Liberties," *World Beyond War*, http://worldbeyondwar.org/liberties.

133   "War Threatens the Environment," *World Beyond War*, http://worldbeyondwar.org/environment.

134   "War Impoverishes," *World Beyond War*, http://worldbeyondwar.org/impoverishes.

135   "We Need $2 Trillion/Year for Other Things," *World Beyond War*, http://worldbeyondwar.org/2trillion.

136   "Ratification of 18 International Human Rights Treaties," *United Nations Human Rights Office of the High Commissioner*, http://indicators.ohchr.org.

137   Pat Elder, "GI Nik Cruz," *World Beyond War*, http://worldbeyondwar.org/gi-nik-cruz (March 5, 2018).

138   "Estimated Number of Guns per Capita by Country," *Wikipedia*, https://en.wikipedia.org/wiki/Estimated_number_of_guns_per_capita_by_country.

139   Jamiles Lartey, "By the numbers: US police kill more in days than other countries do in years," *The Guardian*, https://www.theguardian.com/us-news/2015/jun/09/the-counted-police-killings-us-vs-other-countries (June 9, 2015).

140   "List of Killings by Law Enforcement Officers by Country," *Wikipedia*, https://en.wikipedia.org/wiki/List_of_killings_by_law_enforcement_officers_by_countries.

141   Devon Haynie, "Report: The U.S. is the World's 7th Largest Executioner," *U.S. News & World Report*, https://www.usnews.com/news/best-countries/articles/2017-04-10/report-the-us-is-the-worlds-7th-largest-executioner (April 10, 2017).

142   —Michelle Ye Hee Lee, "Yes, U.S. Locks People Up at a Higher Rate Than Any Other Country," *Washington Post*, https://www.washingtonpost.com/news/fact-checker/wp/2015/07/07/yes-u-s-locks-people-up-at-a-higher-rate-than-any-other-country/?utm_term=.5ea21d773e21 (July 7, 2015). —"List of Countries by Incarceration Rate," *Wikipedia*, https://en.wikipedia.org/wiki/List_of_countries_by_incarceration_rate.

143   Joshua Manson, "UN Report Compares Solitary Confinement Practices in the U.S. and Around the World," *Solitary Watch*, http://solitarywatch.com/2016/10/28/ un-report-compares-solitary-confinement-practices-around-the-world (October 28, 2016).

144   David Swanson, "Talk Nation Radio: Nasim Chatha on Prison Imperialism," *Let's Try Democracy*, http://davidswanson.org/talk-nation-radio-nasim-chatha-on-prison-imperialism (February 6, 2018).

145   Melissa Breyer, "Top 10 Countries Killing the Planet," *Care2*, https://www.care2.com/greenliving/ top-10-countries-ruining-the-planet.html (May 11, 2010).

146   Amir Khan, "America Tops List of 10 Most Obese Countries," *U.S. News & World Report*, https:// health.usnews.com/health-news/health-wellness/ articles/2014/05/28/america-tops-list-of-10-most-obese-countries (May 28, 2014).

147   "The Most Litigious Countries in the World," *Clements Worldwide*, https://www.clements.com/sites/ default/files/resources/The-Most-Litigious-Countries-in-the-World.pdf.

148   "List of Countries by Number of Billionaires," *Wikipedia*, https://en.wikipedia.org/wiki/List_of_ countries_by_the_number_of_billionaires.

149   Kelsey Sheehy, "Undergraduates Around the World Face Student Loan Debt, *U.S. News & World Report*,

https://www.usnews.com/education/best-global-universities/articles/2013/11/13/undergrads-around-the-world-face-student-loan-debt (November 13, 2013).

150   —Ian Graham, "Media: Television viewing: Countries Compared," *Nation Master*, http://www.nationmaster.com/country-info/stats/Media/Television-viewing.
— "Average daily TV viewing time per person in selected countries worldwide in 2016 (in minutes)," *Statista*, https://www.statista.com/statistics/276748/average-daily-tv-viewing-time-per-person-in-selected-countries.

151   "List of Countries by Road Network Size," *Wikipedia*, https://en.wikipedia.org/wiki/List_of_countries_by_road_network_size.

152   "List of Countries by Vehicles per Capita," *Wikipedia*, https://en.wikipedia.org/wiki/List_of_countries_by_vehicles_per_capita.

153   "Food Waste," NRDC, https://www.nrdc.org/issues/food-waste.

154   "Global Food Losses and Food Waste," *Food and Agriculture Organization of the United Nations*, http://www.fao.org/docrep/014/mb060e/mb060e.pdf (2011).

155   Lizzie Dearden, "Top 10 Countries for Cosmetic Surgery Revealed as Figures Show Rising Demand for Penis Enlargements and Other Procedures," *Independent*, https://www.independent.co.uk/life-style/health-and-families/health-news/top-10-countries-for-cosmetic-surgery-revealed-as-figures-show-

industry-is-booming-worldwide-9636861.html (July 30, 2014).

156   Peter Nowak, "U.S. leads the way in porn production, but falls behind in profits," *Canadian Business*, http://www.canadianbusiness.com/blogs-and-comment/u-s-leads-the-way-in-porn-production-but-falls-behind-in-profits (Jan 5, 2012).

157   Deidre McPhillips, "U.S. Among Most Depressed Countries in the World," *U.S. News & World Report*, https://www.usnews.com/news/best-countries/articles/2016-09-14/the-10-most-depressed-countries (September 14, 2016).

158   "Convention on the Elimination of All Forms of Discrimination against Women," *United Nations Treaty Collection*, https://treaties.un.org/Pages/ViewDetails.aspx?src=TREATY&mtdsg_no=IV-8&chapter=4&lang=en.

159   "Every Last Girl," *Save the Children*, https://www.savethechildren.org.uk/content/dam/global/reports/advocacy/every-last-girl.pdf (2016).

160   Mugambi Jouet, *Exceptional America: What Divides Americans from the World and from Each Other* (Oakland: University of California Press, 2017) pp. 137-138.

161   — Steve Crabtree, "Religiosity Highest in World's Poorest Nations," *Gallup*, http://news.gallup.com/poll/142727/religiosity-highest-world-poorest-nations.aspx (August 31, 2010).
— Rick Noack, "Map: These are the world's least

religious countries," *Washington Post*, https://
www.washingtonpost.com/news/worldviews/
wp/2015/04/14/map-these-are-the-worlds-least-
religious-countries/?utm_term=.b918d2b010e4 (April
14, 2015).
—"Importance of Religion by Country," *Wikipedia*,
https://en.wikipedia.org/wiki/Importance_of_religion_
by_country.

162   Mugambi Jouet, *Exceptional America: What
Divides Americans from the World and from Each Other*
(Oakland: University of California Press, 2017) p. 93.

163   Mary Green and Ale Russian, "Oprah Winfrey
Reveals the One Thing That Could Make Her Run
for President," *People Magazine*, http://people.com/
movies/oprah-winfrey-one-thing-make-her-run-
president-exclusive (February 28, 2018).

164   Tom W. Smith and Seokho Kim, "National
Pride in Cross-national and Temporal Perspective,
International Journal of Public Opinion Research, 18
(Spring, 2006), pp. 127-136, http://www-news.
uchicago.edu/releases/06/060301.nationalpride.pdf.

165   Jeffrey M. Jones, "Americans See U.S. as
Exceptional; 37% Doubt Obama Does," *Gallup*, http://
news.gallup.com/poll/145358/americans-exceptional-
doubt-obama.aspx (December 22, 2010).

166   Jerome Karabel and Daniel Laurison, "An
Exceptional Nation? American Political Values in
Comparative Perspective," *IRLE Working Paper,* No. 136-
12, http://irle.berkeley.edu/workingpapers/136-12.pdf

(2012).

167   Tom W. Smith and Seokho Kim, "National Pride in Cross-national and Temporal Perspective, *International Journal of Public Opinion Research*, 18 (Spring, 2006), pp. 127-136, http://www-news. uchicago.edu/releases/06/060301.nationalpride.pdf.

168   Hilde Eliassen Restad, "Are We Coming to the End of 'American Exceptionalism'?," *Newsweek*, http:// www.newsweek.com/are-coming-end-american-exceptionalism-433781 (March 6, 2016).

169   Jeffrey M. Jones, "Americans See U.S. as Exceptional; 37% Doubt Obama Does," *Gallup*, http:// news.gallup.com/poll/145358/americans-exceptional-doubt-obama.aspx (December 22, 2010).

170   Michael D. Shear and Scott Wilson, "On European Trip, President Tries to Set a New, Pragmatic Tone," *Washington Post*, http://www.washingtonpost.com/wp-dyn/content/article/2009/04/04/AR2009040400700. html (April 5, 2009).

171   Mugambi Jouet, *Exceptional America: What Divides Americans from the World and from Each Other* (Oakland: University of California Press, 2017) p. 26.

172   — Stephanie Condon, "Americans split on American exceptionalism, poll shows," *CBS News*, https://www.cbsnews.com/news/americans-split-on-american-exceptionalism-poll-shows (November 18, 2011).
— "Polls: Is America exceptional?," *CNN*, http://

politicalticker.blogs.cnn.com/2013/09/12/polls-is-america-exceptional (September 12, 2013).

173   Peter Moore, "Poll Results: American Exceptionalism," *YouGov*, https://today.yougov.com/news/2013/09/19/poll-results-american-exceptionalism (September 19, 2013).

174   Amy Sullivan, "Millions of Americans Believe God Made Trump President," *Politico*, https://www.politico.com/magazine/story/2018/01/27/millions-of-americans-believe-god-made-trump-president-216537 (January 27, 2018).

175   Seymour Martin Lipset, *American Exceptionalism: A Double-Edged Sword* (New York: W.W. Norton and Company, 1996).

176   Cristina Maza, "Trump Will Start the End of the World, Claim Evangelicals Who Support Him," *Newsweek*, http://www.newsweek.com/trump-will-bring-about-end-worldevangelicals-end-times-779643 (January 12, 2018).

177   John D. Wilsey, *American Exceptionalism and Civil Religion: Reassessing the History of an Idea* (Downers Grove: InterVarsity Press, 2015).

178   — Paula Reed Ward, "DoD paid $53 million of taxpayers' money to pro sports for military tributes, report says," *Pittsburgh Post-Gazette*, https://www.post-gazette.com/news/nation/2015/11/06/Department-of-Defense-paid-53-million-to-pro-sports-for-military-tributes-report-says/

stories/201511060140 (November 6, 2015).
—John McCain and Jeff Flake, "Tackling Paid Patriotism," https://www.mccain.senate.gov/public/_cache/files/12de6dcb-d8d8-4a58-8795-562297f948c1/tackling-paid-patriotism-oversight-report.pdf.

179   "Full text of President Trump's first State of the Union address," *CBS News*, https://www.cbsnews.com/news/2018-state-of-the-union-address-trump-transcript-full-text (January 30, 2018).

180   Mugambi Jouet, *Exceptional America: What Divides Americans from the World and from Each Other* (Oakland: University of California Press, 2017).

181   John D. Wilsey, *American Exceptionalism and Civil Religion: Reassessing the History of an Idea* (Downers Grove: InterVarsity Press, 2015).

182   Herman Melville, *White Jacket; Or, The World on a Man-of-War*, Project Gutenberg, http://www.gutenberg.org/files/10712/10712-h/10712-h.htm.

183   "Full transcript of Pence's Knesset speech," *Jerusalem Post*, http://www.jpost.com/Israel-News/Full-transcript-of-Pences-Knesset-speech-539476 (January 22, 2018).

184   Dick Cheney and Liz Cheney, *Exceptional: Why the World Needs a Powerful America* (Threshold Editions, 2015).

185   "Nobel Lecture by Barack H. Obama, Oslo, 10 December 2009," *NobelPrize.org*, https://www.

nobelprize.org/nobel_prizes/peace/laureates/2009/
obama-lecture_en.html.

186   Norm Dixon, "How Reagan Armed Saddam
with Chemical Weapons," *Counter Punch*, https://www.
counterpunch.org/2004/06/17/how-reagan-armed-
saddam-with-chemical-weapons (June 17, 2004).

187   Dick Cheney and Liz Cheney, *Exceptional: Why
the World Needs a Powerful America* (Threshold Editions,
2015).

188   Seymour Martin Lipset, *American
Exceptionalism: A Double-Edged Sword* (New York: W.W.
Norton and Company, 1996).

189   Seymour Martin Lipset, *American
Exceptionalism: A Double-Edged Sword* (New York: W.W.
Norton and Company, 1996).

190   Jay Parini, "Does American exceptionalism make
us dumb?," *CNN*, http://www.cnn.com/2015/02/24/
opinion/parini-american-exceptionalism/index.html
(February 24, 2015).

191   Seymour Martin Lipset, *American
Exceptionalism: A Double-Edged Sword* (New York: W.W.
Norton and Company, 1996).

192   George Orwell, "Notes on Nationalism," http://
www.orwell.ru/library/essays/nationalism/english/e_
nat.

193   Dick Cheney and Liz Cheney, *Exceptional: Why*

the World Needs a Powerful America (Threshold Editions, 2015).

194   Meredith Bennett-Smith, "Womp! This Country Was Named The Greatest Threat To World Peace," *HuffPost*, https://www.huffingtonpost.com/2014/01/02/greatest-threat-world-peace-country_n_4531824.html (January 23, 2014).

195   Dorothy Manevich and Hanyu Chwe, "Globally, more people see U.S. power and influence as a major threat," *Pew Research Center*, http://www.pewresearch.org/fact-tank/2017/08/01/u-s-power-and-influence-increasingly-seen-as-threat-in-other-countries (August 1, 2017).

196   David Swanson, "U.S. Wars and Hostile Actions: A List," *Let's Try Democracy*, http://davidswanson.org/warlist.

197   David Swanson, "U.S. Wars and Hostile Actions: A List," *Let's Try Democracy*, http://davidswanson.org/warlist.

198   David Swanson, "What Are Foreign Military Bases for?," *Let's Try Democracy*, http://davidswanson.org/what-are-foreign-military-bases-for (July 13, 2015).

199   Phil Stewart, "Ecuador wants military base in Miami," *Reuters*, https://uk.reuters.com/article/ecuador-base/ecuador-wants-military-base-in-miami-idUKADD25267520071022 (October 22, 2007).

200   "The Core International Human Rights

Instruments and their monitoring bodies," *United Nations Human Rights Office of the High Commissioner*, http://www.ohchr.org/EN/ProfessionalInterest/Pages/CoreInstruments.aspx.

201   David Swanson, "Talk Nation Radio: Gareth Porter: Iran Has Never Had a Nuclear Weapons Program," *Let's Try Democracy*, http://davidswanson.org/talk-nation-radio-gareth-porter-iran-has-never-had-a-nuclear-weapons-program-3 (February 12, 2014).

202   David Swanson, "Hiroshima Haunting," *Let's Try Democracy*," http://davidswanson.org/hiroshima-haunting (August 6, 2017).

203   David Swanson, "Video: RT Covers Jeffrey Sterling Trial," *Let's Try Democracy*, http://davidswanson.org/video-rt-covers-jeffrey-sterling-trial-2 (January 16, 2015).

204   "Nuclear Posture Review," U.S. Department of Defense, https://www.defense.gov/News/Special-Reports/NPR.

205   "Al Khamenei's Fatwa Against Nuclear Weapons," *Wikipedia*, https://en.wikipedia.org/wiki/Ali_Khamenei%27s_fatwa_against_nuclear_weapons.

206   Daniel Ellsberg, *The Doomsday Machine: Confessions of a Nuclear War Planner* (Bloomsbury USA , 2017), http://www.ellsberg.net/category/doomsday-machine.

207   Daniel Ellsberg, *The Doomsday Machine:*

Confessions of a Nuclear War Planner (Bloomsbury USA , 2017), http://www.ellsberg.net/category/doomsday-machine.

208   Karl Jacoby, "How exactly is America exceptional?," *Los Angeles Times*, http://www.latimes.com/nation/la-oe-jacoby-american-exceptionalism-ap-tests-20150315-story.html (March 13, 2015).

209   David Swanson, "Books," *Let's Try Democracy*, http://davidswanson.org/books.

210   Walter H. Conser, Jr., Ronald M. McCarthy, David J. Toscano, & Gene Sharp (Eds.), *Resistance, Politics, and the American Struggle for Independence, 1765–1775* (Lynne Rienner, 1986).

211   Luis Fernando Mata Licón, "Do countries other than America do a 'pledge of allegiance' to their flag in school?," *Quora*, https://www.quora.com/Do-countries-other-than-America-do-a-pledge-of-allegiance-to-their-flag-in-school/answer/Luis-Fernando-Mata-Lic%C3%B3n#.

212   "Pledge of Allegiance to the Philippine Flag," *Wikipedia*, https://en.wikipedia.org/wiki/Pledge_of_Allegiance_to_the_Philippine_Flag.

213   "Pledge of Allegiance to the Flag of South Korea," *Wikipedia*, https://en.wikipedia.org/wiki/Pledge_of_Allegiance_to_the_Flag_of_South_Korea.

214   "46 Times President Obama told Americans 'That's Not Who We Are'," *Youtube*, https://www.

youtube.com/watch?v=gouAcayDwLM (November 29, 2015).

215   Frederick Douglass, "What to the Slave Is the Fourth of July?," *TeachingAmericanHistory.org*, http://teachingamericanhistory.org/library/document/what-to-the-slave-is-the-fourth-of-july (July 5, 1852).

216   Langston Hughes, "Let America Be America Again," *Poets.org*, https://www.poets.org/poetsorg/poem/let-america-be-america-again.

217   "Declaration of Independence of the Democratic Republic of Vietnam," *History Matters*, http://historymatters.gmu.edu/d/5139.

218   "Life is cheap in the Orient," *Youtube*, https://www.youtube.com/watch?v=Z9vFzN5MbFk.

219   "Subjects of UN Security Council Vetoes," *Global Policy Forum*, https://www.globalpolicy.org/images/pdfs/Z/Tables_and_Charts/vetosubj.pdf.

220   "Jim Paul on the UN Security Council as a Tool of U.S. Domination," *Let's Try Democracy*, http://davidswanson.org/jim-paul-on-the-un-security-council-as-a-tool-of-u-s-domination (January 9, 2018).

221   David Swanson, "Western Refugee Policies Are One Endless Evian Conference," *Let's Try Democracy*, http://davidswanson.org/western-refugee-policies-are-one-endless-evian-conference (December 14, 2017).

222   David Swanson, "Western Refugee Policies Are

One Endless Evian Conference," *Let's Try Democracy*, http://davidswanson.org/western-refugee-policies-are-one-endless-evian-conference (December 14, 2017).

223   David Swanson, *War Is A Lie*, Second Edition (Charlottesville: Just World Books, 2016).

224   David Swanson, "Western Refugee Policies Are One Endless Evian Conference," *Let's Try Democracy*, http://davidswanson.org/western-refugee-policies-are-one-endless-evian-conference (December 14, 2017).

225   David Swanson, "Western Refugee Policies Are One Endless Evian Conference," *Let's Try Democracy*, http://davidswanson.org/western-refugee-policies-are-one-endless-evian-conference (December 14, 2017).

226   David Swanson, "Western Refugee Policies Are One Endless Evian Conference," *Let's Try Democracy*, http://davidswanson.org/western-refugee-policies-are-one-endless-evian-conference (December 14, 2017).

227   David Swanson, "Western Refugee Policies Are One Endless Evian Conference," *Let's Try Democracy*, http://davidswanson.org/western-refugee-policies-are-one-endless-evian-conference (December 14, 2017).

228   Ervin Birnbaum, "Evian: The Most Fateful Conference of All Times in Jewish History," *Crethi Plethi*, http://www.crethiplethi.com/evian-the-most-fateful-confcrence-of-all-times-in-jewish-history/the-holocaust/2013.

229   "Evian Conference," *Zionism and Israel -*

Encyclopedic Dictionary, http://www.zionism-israel. com/dic/Evian_conference.htm.

230   Nicholson Baker, *Human Smoke: The Beginnings of World War II, the End of Civilization*, (Simon & Schuster, 2009).

231   "MS St. Louis," *Wikipedia*, https://en.wikipedia. org/wiki/MS_St._Louis.

232   Frank Newport, "Historical Review: Americans' Views on Refugees Coming to U.S.," *Gallup*, http:// news.gallup.com/opinion/polling-matters/186716/ historical-review-americans-views-refugees-coming. aspx (November 19, 2015).

233   Elahe Izadi, "Anne Frank and her family were also denied entry as refugees to the U.S.," *Washington Post*, https://www.washingtonpost.com/news/ worldviews/wp/2015/11/24/anne-frank-and-her-family-were-also-denied-entry-as-refugees-to-the-u-s/?utm_term=.f483423866ac (November 24, 2015).

234   "World War II Casualties," *Wikipedia*, https:// en.wikipedia.org/wiki/World_War_II_casualties.

235   James Bradley, *The Imperial Cruise: A Secret History of Empire and War*, (Back Bay Books, 2010).

236   David Swanson, "76 Years of Pearl Harbor Lies," *Let's Try Democracy*, http://davidswanson.org/76-years-of-pearl-harbor-lies (December 7, 2017).

237   David Swanson, "76 Years of Pearl Harbor Lies,"

Let's Try Democracy, http://davidswanson.org/76-years-of-pearl-harbor-lies (December 7, 2017).

238   David Swanson, "76 Years of Pearl Harbor Lies," *Let's Try Democracy*, http://davidswanson.org/76-years-of-pearl-harbor-lies (December 7, 2017).

239   David Swanson, "76 Years of Pearl Harbor Lies," *Let's Try Democracy*, http://davidswanson.org/76-years-of-pearl-harbor-lies (December 7, 2017).

240   David Swanson, "76 Years of Pearl Harbor Lies," *Let's Try Democracy*, http://davidswanson.org/76-years-of-pearl-harbor-lies (December 7, 2017).

241   Daniel Ellsberg, *The Doomsday Machine: Confessions of a Nuclear War Planner* (Bloomsbury USA, 2017), http://www.ellsberg.net/category/doomsday-machine.

242   Dick Cheney and Liz Cheney, *Exceptional: Why the World Needs a Powerful America* (Threshold Editions, 2015).

243   Dick Cheney and Liz Cheney, *Exceptional: Why the World Needs a Powerful America* (Threshold Editions, 2015).

244   Ewen MacAskill, *The Guardian,* "Fivefold increase in terrorism fatalities since 9/11, says report," https://www.theguardian.com/uk-news/2014/nov/18/fivefold-increase-terrorism-fatalities-global-index (November 17, 2014).

245   Global Terrorism Index, http://
globalterrorismindex.org.

246   Martin Luther King Jr., "Beyond Vietnam,"
http://kingencyclopedia.stanford.edu/encyclopedia/
documentsentry/doc_beyond_vietnam (April 4, 1967).

247   Sam Husseini, "Commenting on Orlando, NPR
Terrorism Reporter Reverses Political Lesson of Madrid
Blast," *Fairness and Accuracy in Reporting (FAIR),*
https://fair.org/home/commenting-on-orlando-npr-
terrorism-reporter-reverses-political-lesson-of-madrid-
blast (June 13, 2016).

248   Adam Taylor, "It's not just Hiroshima: The many
other things America hasn't apologized for," *Washington
Post,* https://www.washingtonpost.com/news/
worldviews/wp/2016/05/26/the-things-america-
hasnt-apologized-for/?utm_term=.b22fbb902a83 (May
26, 2016).

249   Adam Taylor, "It's not just Hiroshima: The many
other things America hasn't apologized for," *Washington
Post,* https://www.washingtonpost.com/news/
worldviews/wp/2016/05/26/the-things-america-
hasnt-apologized-for/?utm_term=.b22fbb902a83 (May
26, 2016).

250   Peter Baker, "Obama Apologizes After Drone
Kills American and Italian Held by Al Qaeda," *New York
Times,* https://www.nytimes.com/2015/04/24/world/
asia/2-qaeda-hostages-were-accidentally-killed-in-us-
raid-white-house-says.html (April 23, 2015).

251   Jo Becker and Scott Shane, "Secret 'Kill List' Proves a Test of Obama's Principles and Will," *New York Times*, http://www.nytimes.com/2012/05/29/world/obamas-leadership-in-war-on-al-qaeda.html (May 29, 2012).

252   Ian Murphy, "Obama Brags He's 'Really Good at Killing People,'" *The Progressive*, http://progressive.org/dispatches/obama-brags-really-good-killing-people (November 4, 2013).

253   Glenn Greenwald, "Obama Killed a 16-Year-Old American in Yemen. Trump Just Killed His 8-Year-Old Sister," *The Intercept*, https://theintercept.com/2017/01/30/obama-killed-a-16-year-old-american-in-yemen-trump-just-killed-his-8-year-old-sister (January 30 2017).

254   "Ron Paul Booed by Insane Debate Audience for Endorsing the Golden Rule," *Youtube*, https://www.youtube.com/watch?v=7v8qtZ3I5AM.

255   Hilde Eliassen Restad, *American Exceptionalism: An Idea that Made a Nation and Remade the World* (Routledge, 2014).

256   Hilde Eliassen Restad, *American Exceptionalism: An Idea that Made a Nation and Remade the World* (Routledge, 2014).

257   Dick Cheney and Liz Cheney, *Exceptional: Why the World Needs a Powerful America* (Threshold Editions, 2015).

258   "Philippine American War,"
Wikipedia, https://en.wikipedia.org/wiki/
Philippine%E2%80%93American_War.

259   "Philippine American War,"
Wikipedia, https://en.wikipedia.org/wiki/
Philippine%E2%80%93American_War.

260   Brenda Wineapple, "The Large Policy: How
the Spanish-American War laid the groundwork for
American empire," *The Nation*, https://www.thenation.
com/article/how-the-spanish-american-war-laid-the-
groundwork-for-american-empire (January 31, 2018).

261   James Bradley, *The Imperial Cruise: A Secret
History of Empire and War*, (Back Bay Books, 2010).

262   Ray Raphael, *Founding Myths: Stories That Hide
Our Patriotic Past* (New York: MJF Books, 2004).

263   Franklin Roosevelt, "1941 State of the Union
Address," http://voicesofdemocracy.umd.edu/fdr-the-
four-freedoms-speech-text (January 6, 1941).

264   Andrew Kohut and Bruce Stokes, "The Problem
of American Exceptionalism," *Pew Research Center*,
http://www.pewresearch.org/2006/05/09/the-
problem-of-american-exceptionalism (May 9, 2006).

265   Christopher Preble, "How Americans Feel About
Going to (Nuclear) War," *War on the Rocks*, https://
warontherocks.com/2017/08/how-americans-feel-
about-going-to-nuclear-war (August 15, 2017).

266   Nicolas J.S. Davies, "The Illusion of War Without Casualties," *Consortium News*, https://consortiumnews.com/2018/03/09/the-illusion-of-war-without-casualties (March 9, 2018).

267   "Public Says It's Illegal to Target Americans Abroad As Some Question CIA Drone Attacks," *AHHerald.com*, http://www.ahherald.com/newsbrief-mainmenu-2/monmouth-county-news/14849-public-says-its-illegal-to-target-americans-abroad-as-some-question-cia-drone-attacks (February 7, 2013).

268   Marjorie Cohn, "Pentagon to Allow Nuclear Responses to Non-Nuclear Attacks," *Truthout*, http://www.truth-out.org/news/item/43460-pentagon-to-allow-nuclear-responses-to-non-nuclear-attacks (February 6, 2018).

269   While the U.S. has typically paid $0 to $5,000 dollars as compensation for an Iraqi life, (see http://www.informationclearinghouse.info/article18576.htm) the State Department and Blackwater arrived at the figure of $15,000, (see http://scienceblogs.com/authority/2007/10/08/how-much-is-an-iraqi-life-wort). At the same time, the lowest government value for a U.S. life was $5 million assigned by the Food and Drug Administration, (see http://www.nytimes.com/2011/02/17/business/economy/17regulation.html?pagewanted=all).

270   "Harry S. Truman," *Wikipedia*, https://en.wikipedia.org/wiki/Harry_S._Truman#cite_ref-84.

271   "Madeleine Albright - The deaths of 500,000

Iraqi children was worth it for Iraq's non existent WMD's," *Youtube*, https://www.youtube.com/watch?v=RM0uvgHKZe8.

272   Jon Greenberg, "Most people clueless on U.S. foreign aid spending," *Politifact*, http://www.politifact.com/global-news/statements/2016/nov/09/john-kerry/yep-most-people-clueless-us-foreign-aid-spending (November 9, 2016).

273   Kevin Robillard, "Poll: Most only want foreign aid cuts," *Politico*, https://www.politico.com/story/2013/02/poll-most-only-want-foreign-aid-cuts-087948 (February 22, 2013).

274   David Swanson, "Ever More Shocked, Never Yet Awed," *Let's Try Democracy*, http://davidswanson.org/iraq (March 18, 2013).

275   Hilde Eliassen Restad, "Are We Coming to the End of 'American Exceptionalism'?," *Newsweek*, http://www.newsweek.com/are-coming-end-american-exceptionalism-433781 (March 6, 2016).

276   — Lucia Newman, "Castro: U.S. hasn't responded to Katrina offer," *CNN*, http://www.cnn.com/2005/WORLD/americas/09/05/katrina.cuba (September 5, 2005).
— "Despite oil donations, offers of Katrina aid, Chavez never caught on as savior of poor in US," *Associated Press*, http://www.foxnews.com/weather/2013/03/07/despite-oil-donations-offers-katrina-aid-chavez-never-caught-on-as-savior-poor (March 7, 2013).

277   Jeffrey M. Jones, "Democratic, Republican Identification Near Historical Lows," *Gallup*, http://news.gallup.com/poll/188096/democratic-republican-identification-near-historical-lows.aspx (January 11, 2016).

278   David Swanson, "Trump's Articles of Impeachment: A Greatest Hits Collection," *Let's Try Democracy*, http://davidswanson.org/firedonaldtrump (August 23, 2017).

279   Amy B Wang, "Trump asked for a 'Muslim ban,' Giuliani says — and ordered a commission to do it 'legally'," *Washington Post*, https://www.washingtonpost.com/news/the-fix/wp/2017/01/29/trump-asked-for-a-muslim-ban-giuliani-says-and-ordered-a-commission-to-do-it-legally/?utm_term=.b68f73002e02 (January 29, 2017).

280   David Brody, "Brody File Exclusive: President Trump Says Persecuted Christians Will Be Given Priority As Refugees," *CBN News*, http://www1.cbn.com/thebrodyfile/archive/2017/01/27/brody-file-exclusive-president-trump-says-persecuted-christians-will-be-given-priority-as-refugees (January 27, 2017).

281   Matt Zapotosky, "A new travel ban with 'mostly minor technical differences'? That probably won't cut it, analysts say," *Washington Post*, https://www.washingtonpost.com/world/national-security/a-new-travel-ban-with-mostly-minor-technical-differences-that-probably-wont-cut-it-analysts-say/2017/02/22/8ae9d7e6-f918-11e6-bf01-d47f8cf9b643_story.html?utm_term=.fabc81c941cb

(February 22, 2017).

282   Jake Miller, "Donald Trump defends calling Mexican immigrants 'rapists,'" *CBS News*, https://www.cbsnews.com/news/election-2016-donald-trump-defends-calling-mexican-immigrants-rapists (July 2, 2015).

283   Willa Frej, "Joe Arpaio's 'Concentration Camp' Is Finally Closed: There's a new sheriff in town," *HuffPost*, https://www.huffingtonpost.com/entry/joe-arpaio-tent-city-closed_us_59ddcdafe4b04fc4e1e9f01a (October 11, 2017).

284   "Brandenburg v. Ohio," *Wikipedia*, https://en.wikipedia.org/wiki/Brandenburg_v._Ohio.

285   Sam Reisman, "Trump Tells Crowd to 'Knock the Crap Out' of Protesters, Offers to Pay Legal Fees," *Mediaite*, https://www.mediaite.com/online/trump-tells-crowd-to-knock-the-crap-out-of-protesters-offers-to-pay-legal-fees (February 1, 2016).

286   Robert Mackey, "Trump Concerned His Rallies Are Not Violent Enough," *The Intercept*, https://theintercept.com/2016/03/11/trumps-good-old-days-when-battering-protesters-was-celebrated-in-the-white-house (March 11 2016).

287   Michael Finnegan and Noah Bierman, "Trump's endorsement of violence reaches new level: He may pay legal fees for assault suspect," *Los Angeles Times*, http://www.latimes.com/politics/la-na-trump-campaign-protests-20160313-story.html (March 13, 2016).

288   Jonathan Lemire, "Trump blames 'many sides' after violent white supremacist rally in Virginia," *Associated Press*, http://www.chicagotribune.com/ news/nationworld/politics/ct-trump-charlottesville-violence-20170812-story.html (August 13, 2017).

289   Biodiversivist, "European biodiesel industry being bankrupted by loophole," *Grist*, https://grist.org/ politics/donald-trump-climate-action-new-york-times (April 3, 2008).

290   "Policy Paper on Case Selection," *International Criminal Court Office of the Prosecutor*, https://www.icc-cpi.int/itemsDocuments/20160915_OTP-Policy_Case-Selection_Eng.pdf (September 15, 2016).

291   Donald Trump, "Presidential Executive Order on Establishing Discipline and Accountability in the Environmental Review and Permitting Process for Infrastructure," *White House*, https://www.whitehouse. gov/presidential-actions/presidential-executive-order-establishing-discipline-accountability-environmental-review-permitting-process-infrastructure (August 15, 2017).

292   — Dominique Mosbergen, "Half Of Hurricane Harvey Victims Say FEMA Application Was Denied Or Is Still Pending," *HuffPost*, https://www.huffingtonpost. com/entry/harvey-fema-application-denied-survey_us_5a27a8cae4b02d3bfc368aab (December 6, 2017). — Joel Achenbach, "Only 26 percent of Hurricane Harvey survivors had FEMA aid request approved, survey finds," *Washington Post*, https://www.washingtonpost.

com/news/post-nation/wp/2017/12/05/
only-26-percent-of-hurricane-harvey-survivors-
have-had-fema-aid-request-approved-survey-
finds/?utm_term=.44dc8c3b8209 (December 5, 2017).

293   Jennifer Rubin, "Did Trump just figure out
that Puerto Ricans are Americans?," *Washington
Post*, https://www.washingtonpost.com/blogs/
right-turn/wp/2017/09/26/did-trump-just-
figure-out-that-puerto-ricans-are-americans/?utm_
term=.216c8d167702 (September 26, 2017).

294   David Ignatius, "An Opening for the Democrats,"
Washington Post, http://www.washingtonpost.com/wp-
dyn/content/article/2007/01/11/AR2007011101575.
html (January 12, 2007).

295   Heather Caygle, "Pelosi moves to muzzle Trump
impeachment talk," *Politico*, https://www.politico.
com/story/2017/11/01/trump-impeachment-talk-
pelosi-244336 (November 1, 2017).

296   John Nichols, *The Genius of Impeachment* (New
Press, 2006).

297   David Swanson, "Newsweek Poll Shows Majority
Supports Impeachment," *War Is A Crime*, http://old.
warisacrime.org/node/14897.

298   "Russian 'meddling' as bad as Pearl Harbor
attack, some US pundits claim," *RT*, https://www.
rt.com/usa/419263-russian-meddling-pearl-harbor
(February 22, 2018).

299   Oren Dorell, "Russia's pattern of meddling abroad exposes threat to 2018 U.S. elections: report," *USA Today*, https://www.usatoday.com/story/news/world/2018/01/10/russias-pattern-meddling-money-laundering-and-murder-influence-abroad-poses-threat-2018-u-s-election/1019012001 (January 10, 2018).

300   David E. Sanger and William J. Broadjan, "Pentagon Suggests Countering Devastating Cyberattacks With Nuclear Arms," *New York Times*, https://www.nytimes.com/2018/01/16/us/politics/pentagon-nuclear-review-cyberattack-trump.html (January 16, 2018).

301   Hilary Hanson, "Leaked Emails Suggest DNC Was Conspiring Against Bernie Sanders," *HuffPost*, https://www.huffingtonpost.com/entry/wikileaks-dnc-bernie-sanders_us_579381fbe4b02d5d5ed1d157 (July 26, 2016).

302   Nicholas Confessore and Karen Yourish, "$2 Billion Worth of Free Media for Donald Trump," *New York Times*, https://www.nytimes.com/2016/03/16/upshot/measuring-donald-trumps-mammoth-advantage-in-free-media.html (March 15, 2016).

303   Greg Palast, "The GOP's Stealth War Against Voters," *Rolling Stone*, https://www.rollingstone.com/politics/features/the-gops-stealth-war-against-voters-w435890 (August 24, 2016).

304   Monica Davey, Julie Bosman, and Steve Ederdec, "Trump Backers Go to Court to Block Vote Recounts in 3 States," *New York Times*, https://www.nytimes.

com/2016/12/02/us/trump-recounts-wisconsin-michigan-pennsylvania.html (December 2, 2016).

305   Richard Perez-Penadec, "Donald Trump Completes Final Lap, Electoral College, to White House," *New York Times*, https://www.nytimes.com/2016/12/19/us/politics/electoral-college-vote.html (December 19, 2016).

306   Jeff Cohen, "TV Networks Should Open Up the Presidential Debates," *RootsAction*, http://rootsaction.org/news-a-views/1261-tv-networks-should-open-up-the-presidential-debates (August 15, 2016).

307   "Citizens United v. FEC," *Wikipedia*, https://en.wikipedia.org/wiki/Citizens_United_v._FEC.

308   "Make Voter Registration Automatic in Your State Too," *RootsAction*, https://act.rootsaction.org/p/dia/action4/common/public/?action_KEY=12916.

309   Matthew Rozsa, "Voter ID laws contributed to Hillary Clinton's loss in crucial swing states," *Salon*, https://www.salon.com/2016/12/19/voter-id-laws-contributed-to-hillary-clintons-loss-in-crucial-swing-states (December 19, 2016).

310   David Swanson, "How I Produce Fake News for Russia," *Let's Try Democracy*, http://davidswanson.org/how-i-produce-fake-news-for-russia (November 27, 2016).

311   David Swanson, "U.S. Wars and Hostile Actions: A List," *Let's Try Democracy*, http://davidswanson.org/

warlist.

312   Andrey Ostroukh, "Russia Says U.S. Missiles In Poland, Romania Would Violate Treaty," *Reuters*, https://www.huffingtonpost.com/entry/russia-says-us-missiles-in-poland-romania-would-violate-treaty_us_5904cb41e4b05c39767feb0f (April 29, 2017).

313   Stepan Kravchenko, Henry Meyer, and Margaret Talev, "U.S. Strikes Killed Scores of Russia Fighters in Syria, Sources Say," *Bloomberg*, https://www.bloomberg.com/news/articles/2018-02-13/u-s-strikes-said-to-kill-scores-of-russian-fighters-in-syria (February 13, 2018).

314   Robert Parry, "Neocons and the Ukraine Coup," *Consortium News*, https://consortiumnews.com/2014/02/23/neocons-and-the-ukraine-coup (February 23, 2014).

315   One example from the voluminous genre of gridlock stories: Liz Halloran, "What's Really Causing Gridlock In Washington?," *National Public Radio (NPR)*, https://www.npr.org/2011/07/05/137524823/whats-really-causing-gridlock-in-washington (July 4, 2011).

316   Patricia Zengerle, "Senate backs massive increase in military spending," *Reuters*, https://www.reuters.com/article/us-usa-defense-congress/senate-backs-massive-increase-in-military-spending-idUSKCN1BT2PV (September 18, 2017).

317   Trevor Timm, "Democrats Just Handed Trump More Domestic Surveillance Powers. They Should Know

Better," *NBC News*, https://www.commondreams.org/views/2018/01/11/democrats-just-handed-trump-more-domestic-surveillance-powers-they-should-know (January 11, 2018).

318   Mark Perry, "The U.S. Army's War Over Russia," *Politico*, http://www.politico.com/magazine/story/2016/05/army-internal-fight-russia-defense-budget-213885 (May 12, 2016).

319   Jerome Karabel and Daniel Laurison. (2012). "An Exceptional Nation? American Political Values in Comparative Perspective," IRLE Working Paper No. 136-12. http://irle.berkeley.edu/an-exceptional-nation-american-political-values-in-comparative-perspective.

320   David Swanson, "Gallup: U.S. Population Highly Militaristic," *Let's Try Democracy*, http://davidswanson.org/gallup-u-s-population-highly-militaristic (March 17, 2015).

321   "NRA Charlie Daniels Commercial," *Youtube*, https://www.youtube.com/watch?v=xh8vFNynb_w.

322   Edward Luttwak, "It's Time to Bomb North Korea: Destroying Pyongyang's nuclear arsenal is still in America's national interest," *Foreign Policy*, https://foreignpolicy.com/2018/01/08/its-time-to-bomb-north-korea (January 8, 2018).

323   Sarah Lazare, "Observers Slam CNN for Aiding and Abetting Hate Speech in GOP Debate," *Common Dreams*, https://www.commondreams.org/news/2015/12/16/observers-slam-cnn-aiding-and-

abetting-hate-speech-gop-debate (December 16, 2015).

324   Phil Stewart, "Mattis: U.S. isn't widening role in Syria's war, despite strikes," *Reuters*, https://www. reuters.com/article/mideast-crisis-syria-mattis/mattis-u-s-isnt-widening-role-in-syrias-war-despite-strikes-idUSL2N1IK25B (May 18, 2017).

325   Ben Brimelow, "A Russian fighter jet got so aggressive while intercepting a US Navy spy plane that the crew felt 'violent turbulence'," *Business Insider*, http://www.businessinsider.com/aggressive-russia-military-jet-us-navy-black-sea-2018-2 (February 1, 2018).

326   "US tanks arrive in Germany to help Nato defences," *BBC*, http://www.bbc.com/news/world-europe-38537689 (January 6, 2017).

327   Meredith Bennett-Smith, "Womp! This Country Was Named The Greatest Threat To World Peace," *HuffPost*, https://www.huffingtonpost. com/2014/01/02/greatest-threat-world-peace-country_n_4531824.html (January 23, 2014).

328   "Ron Paul Booed by Insane Debate Audience for Endorsing the Golden Rule," *Youtube*, https://www. youtube.com/watch?v=7v8qtZ3I5AM.

329   Richard Wike, Jacob Poushter and Hani Zainulbhai, "America's international image: As Obama Years Draw to Close, President and U.S. Seen Favorably in Europe and Asia," *Pew Research Center*, http://www. pewglobal.org/2016/06/28/americas-international-

image (June 28, 2016).

330   David Ignatius, "In Syria, U.S. credibility is at stake," *Washington Post*, https://www.washingtonpost.com/opinions/david-ignatius-in-syria-us-credibility-is-at-stake/2013/08/28/54e8bc50-0ffd-11e3-bdf6-e4fc677d94a1_story.html?utm_term=.2e66e21ea660 (August 28, 2013).

331   "U.S. Military," *PollingReport.com*, http://www.pollingreport.com/military.htm.

332   David Swanson, "Orlando Killer's Secret Shared by Other Terrorists," *Let's Try Democracy*, http://davidswanson.org/orlando-killers-secret-shared-by-other-terrorists (June 16, 2016).

333   Mugambi Jouet, *Exceptional America: What Divides Americans from the World and from Each Other* (Oakland: University of California Press, 2017) p. 249.

334   "U.S. Flag Recalled After Causing 143 Million Deaths," *The Onion*, https://politics.theonion.com/u-s-flag-recalled-after-causing-143-million-deaths-1819571445 (April 13, 2010).

335   David Swanson, "Videos of Take-A-Knee Discussion of Racism and Militarism," *Let's Try Democracy*, http://davidswanson.org/videos-of-take-a-knee-discussion-of-racism-and-militarism (March 11, 2018).

336   Pat Elder, "JROTC, Military Indoctrination and the Training of Mass Killers," *World Beyond War*, http://

worldbeyondwar.org/jrotc-military-indoctrination-training-mass-killers (February 16, 2018).

337   David Swanson, "U.S. Mass Shooters Are Disproportionately Veterans," *Let's Try Democracy*, http://davidswanson.org/u-s-mass-shooters-are-disproportionately-veterans (November 14, 2017).

338   David Swanson, "Can the Climate Survive Adherence to War and Partisanship?," *Let's Try Democracy*, http://davidswanson.org/can-the-climate-survive-adherence-to-war-and-partisanship (February 16, 2017).

339   Cindy Sheehan and Rick Sterling, "The Missing Message in the Women's March," *Resumen*, http://worldbeyondwar.org/missing-message-womens-march (January 18, 2018).

340   "War Threatens the Environment," *World Beyond War*, http://worldbeyondwar.org/environment.

341   "War Impoverishes," *World Beyond War*, http://worldbeyondwar.org/impoverishes.

342   "War Endangers Us," *World Beyond War*, http://worldbeyondwar.org/endangers.

343   "War Erodes Liberties," *World Beyond War*, http://worldbeyondwar.org/liberties.

344   "War Erodes Liberties," *World Beyond War*, http://worldbeyondwar.org/liberties.

345   Avery Anapol, "Student suspended for sitting through Pledge of Allegiance sues her high school," *The Hill*, http://thehill.com/blogs/blog-briefing-room/354759-student-suspending-for-sitting-through-pledge-of-allegiance-sues-her (October 10, 2017).

346   Donald Trump, "If NFL fans refuse to go to games until players stop disrespecting our Flag & Country, you will see change take place fast. Fire or suspend!," *Twitter*, https://twitter.com/realDonaldTrump/status/911904261553950720 (September 24, 2017).

347   Michael Stone, "Alabama Pastor: People Not Standing For National Anthem Should Be Shot," *Patheos*, http://www.patheos.com/blogs/progressivesecularhumanist/2016/09/alabama-pastor-people-not-standing-for-national-anthem-should-be-shot (September 10, 2016).

348   Cody Benjamin, "2018 Olympics: Mike Pence doesn't stand for Korea, skips meal with North Koreans," *CBS Sports*, https://www.cbssports.com/olympics/news/2018-olympics-mike-pence-doesnt-stand-for-korea-skips-meal-with-north-koreans (February 9, 2018).

349   "Bellamy Salute," *Wikipedia*, https://en.wikipedia.org/wiki/Bellamy_salute.

350   —Christopher Petrella, "The ugly history of the Pledge of Allegiance — and why it matters," *Washington Post*, https://www.washingtonpost.com/news/made-by-history/wp/2017/11/03/the-ugly-history-of-the-pledge-of-allegiance-and-why-it-matters/?utm_term=.

eb612553df5b (November 3, 2017).
—"16 Things That Europeans Find Weird About American Culture," *Providr*, https://www.providr.com/things-europeans-find-weird-about-americans/3 (June 1, 2017).

351   Joseph Carroll, "Public Support for Constitutional Amendment on Flag Burning," *Gallup*, http://news.gallup.com/poll/23524/Public-Support-Constitutional-Amendment-Flag-Burning.aspx (June 29, 2006).

352   —Paula Reed Ward, "DoD paid $53 million of taxpayers' money to pro sports for military tributes, report says," *Pittsburgh Post-Gazette*, https://www.post-gazette.com/news/nation/2015/11/06/Department-of-Defense-paid-53-million-to-pro-sports-for-military-tributes-report-says/stories/201511060140 (November 6, 2015).
—John McCain and Jeff Flake, "Tackling Paid Patriotism," https://www.mccain.senate.gov/public/_cache/files/12de6dcb-d8d8-4a58-8795-562297f948c1/tackling-paid-patriotism-oversight-report.pdf.

353   David Swanson, "Videos of Take-A-Knee Discussion of Racism and Militarism," *Let's Try Democracy*, http://davidswanson.org/videos-of-take-a-knee-discussion-of-racism-and-militarism (March 11, 2018).

354   Jon Schwarz, "Colin Kaepernick Is Righter Than You Know: The National Anthem Is a Celebration of Slavery," *The Intercept*, https://theintercept.com/2016/08/28/colin-kaepernick-is-righter-than-

you-know-the-national-anthem-is-a-celebration-of-slavery (August 28, 2016).

355   John Beacham, "Real history: Star-Spangled Banner made anthem to keep America racist," *Liberation,* https://www.liberationnews.org/real-history-star-spangled-banner-made-anthem-keep-america-racist (August 31, 2017).

356   Jon Schwarz, "Colin Kaepernick Is Righter Than You Know: The National Anthem Is a Celebration of Slavery," *The Intercept*, https://theintercept.com/2016/08/28/colin-kaepernick-is-righter-than-you-know-the-national-anthem-is-a-celebration-of-slavery (August 28, 2016).

357   David Swanson, "Can Canada Get Out of the War Business?," *Let's Try Democracy*, http://davidswanson.org/can-canada-get-out-of-the-war-business (February 27, 2017).

358   "Iraq attack likely 'only if provoked'," *BBC*, http://news.bbc.co.uk/2/hi/middle_east/2312369.stm (October 9, 2002).

359   "Demographics of North Korea," *Wikipedia*, https://en.wikipedia.org/wiki/Demographics_of_North_Korea.

360   Fred Branfman and David Swanson, "Even The Warriors Say The Wars Make Us Less Safe," *Let's Try Democracy*, http://worldbeyondwar.org/lesssafe.

361   Mary Brophy Marcus, "The top 10 leading causes

of death in the U.S.," *CBS News,* https://www.cbsnews.com/news/the-leading-causes-of-death-in-the-us (June 30, 2016).

362   "Most protesters arrested on Inauguration Day will face felony rioting charges, federal prosecutors say," *CBS/AP*, https://www.cbsnews.com/news/inauguration-day-protests-felony-rioting-charges-federal-prosecutors-say (January 21, 2017).

363   David Swanson, *Daybreak: Undoing the Imperial Presidency and Forming a More Perfect Union* (New York: Seven Stories, 2009).

364   "Debate: Syria, Ghouta, and the Left (2/2)," *TheRealNews.com, Youtube*, https://youtu.be/EFirpk8twmY (March 11, 2018).

365   David Swanson, *War Is Never Just* (Charlottesville: David Swanson, 2016).

366   "Statistic on Billboard Explained," *World Beyond War*, http://worldbeyondwar.org/explained.

367   "Inside the U.S. Military Recruitment Program That Trained Nikolas Cruz to Be 'A Very Good Shot'," *Democracy Now*, http://worldbeyondwar.org/inside-u-s-military-recruitment-program-trained-nikolas-cruz-good-shot (February 21, 2018).

368   Steve Wyche, "Colin Kaepernick explains why he sat during national anthem," *NFL*, http://www.nfl.com/news/story/0ap3000000691077/article/colin-kaepernick-explains-why-he-sat-during-national-

anthem (Aug. 28, 2016).

369 "Muhammad Ali refuses to fight in Vietnam (1967)," *Alpha History*, http://alphahistory.com/vietnamwar/muhammad-ali-refuses-to-fight-1967.

370 Martin Luther King, Jr., "Beyond Vietnam," *King Encyclopedia*, http://kingencyclopedia.stanford.edu/encyclopedia/documentsentry/doc_beyond_vietnam (April 4, 1967).

371 John Lennon, "Imagine," *Youtube*, https://www.youtube.com/watch?v=yRhq-yO1KN8.

372 David Swanson, "Videos of Take-A-Knee Discussion of Racism and Militarism," *Let's Try Democracy*, http://davidswanson.org/videos-of-take-a-knee-discussion-of-racism-and-militarism (March 11, 2018).

373 John Donne, "For whom the bell tolls," *Famous Literary Works*, http://www.famousliteraryworks.com/donne_for_whom_the_bell_tolls.htm.

374 This scenarios was suggested to me by this book: Yuval Noah Harari, *Sapiens: A Brief History of Humankind Paperback* (Harper Perennial, 2018).

375 Andrew Prokop, "The 'shithouse defense,' explained: how Trump's allies are trying to dig him out of his 'shithole'," *Vox*, https://www.vox.com/2018/1/16/16897016/trump-shithole-shithouse-countries

376   https://www.nytimes.com/2017/08/08/world/asia/north-korea-un-sanctions-nuclear-missile-united-nations.html (January 16, 2018).

377   Marlise Simons, "Marshall Islands Can't Sue the World's Nuclear Powers, U.N. Court Rules," *New York Times*, https://www.nytimes.com/2016/10/06/world/asia/marshall-islands-un-court-nuclear-disarmament.html (October 5, 2016).

378   David Caplan, Katherine Faulders, "Trump denies telling widow of fallen soldier, 'He knew what he signed up for,'" *ABC News*, http://abcnews.go.com/Politics/trump-denies-telling-widow-fallen-soldier-knew-signed/story?id=50549664 (October 18, 2017).

379   Jodi Rudoren, "Israel Backs Limited Strike Against Syria," *New York Times*, http://www.nytimes.com/2013/09/06/world/middleeast/israel-backs-limited-strike-against-syria.html?pagewanted=all (September 5, 2013).

380   Mary Brophy Marcus, "The top 10 leading causes of death in the U.S.," *CBS News,* https://www.cbsnews.com/news/the-leading-causes-of-death-in-the-us (June 30, 2016).

381   David Swanson, "Ever More Shocked, Never Yet Awed," *Let's Try Democracy*, http://davidswanson.org/iraq (March 18, 2013).

382   Charles Q. Choi, "Geoengineering Ineffective Against Climate Change, Could Make Worse," *Live Science*, https://www.livescience.com/43654-

geoengineering-ineffective-against-climate-change.html
(February 25, 2014).

383   Kayla Zacharias, "Tesla in space could carry
bacteria from Earth," *Purdue University*, https://www.
purdue.edu/newsroom/releases/2018/Q1/tesla-in-
space-could-carry-bacteria-from-earth.html (February
27, 2018).

384   Karen Attiah, "What if Western media covered
Charlottesville the same way it covers other nations,"
Washington Post, https://www.washingtonpost.com/
news/global-opinions/wp/2017/08/16/what-if-
western-media-covered-americas-white-tribalism-
the-same-way-it-covers-other-nations/?utm_term=.
d28908434425 (August 16, 2017).

385   Mirren Gidda, "Most Terrorists in the U.S. Are
Right Wing, Not Muslim: Report," *Newsweek*, http://
www.newsweek.com/right-wing-extremism-islamist-
terrorism-donald-trump-steve-bannon-628381 (June
22, 2017).

386   Karen Attiah, "What if Western media covered
Las Vegas the same way it covers foreign nations?,"
Washington Post, https://www.washingtonpost.com/
news/global-opinions/wp/2017/10/06/what-if-
western-media-covered-las-vegas-the-same-way-it-
covers-foreign-nations/?utm_term=.b2f4f5a6b2b1
(October 6, 2017).

387   "Gunman's Girlfriend Arrives in U.S. and Is
Expected to Be Questioned," *New York Times*, https://

www.nytimes.com/2017/10/03/us/las-vegas-shooting-live-updates.html (October 3, 2017).

388   Scott McLean, Holly Yan, Faith Karimi and Steve Almasy, "Las Vegas killer fired at airport fuel tank," *CNN*, http://www.cnn.com/2017/10/05/us/las-vegas-shooting-investigation/index.html (October 5, 2017).

389   Richard Glover, "How Australia beat the gun lobby and passed gun control," *Washington Post*, https://www.washingtonpost.com/news/global-opinions/wp/2017/10/03/how-australia-beat-the-gun-lobby-and-passed-gun-control/?utm_term=.d62870f37ce4 (October 3, 2017).

390   Steve Rendall, "In Prelude to War, TV Served as Official Megaphone," *Fairness and Accuracy in Reporting (FAIR)*, https://fair.org/extra/in-prelude-to-war-tv-served-as-official-megaphone (April 2003).

391   "United States and Weapons of Mass Destruction," *Wikipedia*, https://en.wikipedia.org/wiki/United_States_and_weapons_of_mass_destruction.

392   Norm Dixon, "How Reagan Armed Saddam with Chemical Weapons," *Counter Punch*, https://www.counterpunch.org/2004/06/17/how-reagan-armed-saddam-with-chemical-weapons (June 17, 2004).

393   David Swanson, "Obama Badly Wanted to Bomb Syria Last Year," *Let's Try Democracy*, http://davidswanson.org/obama-badly-wanted-to-bomb-syria-last-year-4 (May 13, 2014).

394   "Naturalization Oath of Allegiance to the United States of America," *U.S. Citizenship and Immigration Services*, https://www.uscis.gov/us-citizenship/naturalization-test/naturalization-oath-allegiance-united-states-america.

395   "The World Passport," *World Government of World Citizens*, http://worldservice.org/docpass.html.

396   Cover photo for this book: https://www.pexels.com/photo/3d-above-atmosphere-beam-262591.